Stories From Hans Andersen

1911a

'I have hardly closed my eyes the whole night! Heaven knows what was in the bed. I seemed to be lying upon some hard thing, and my whole body is black and blue this morning. It is terrible!'—(Page 113.)

STORIES *FROM* HANS ANDERSEN

WITH ILLUSTRATIONS BY
EDMUND DULAC

HODDER & STOUGHTON
NEW YORK & LONDON

Printed in 1911

ILLUSTRATIONS

THE SNOW QUEEN

ILLUSTRATIONS

THE NIGHTINGALE

THE REAL PRINCESS

ILLUSTRATIONS

THE GARDEN OF PARADISE

THE MERMAID

ILLUSTRATIONS

THE EMPEROR'S NEW CLOTHES

THE WIND'S TALE

THE SNOW QUEEN

A TALE IN SEVEN STORIES

FIRST STORY

WHICH DEALS WITH A MIRROR AND ITS FRAGMENTS

NOW we are about to begin, and you must attend; and when we get to the end of the story, you will know more than you do now about a very wicked hobgoblin. He was one of the worst kind; in fact he was a real demon. One day he was in a high state of delight because he had invented a mirror with this peculiarity, that every good and pretty thing reflected in it shrank away to almost nothing. On the other hand, every bad and good-for-nothing thing stood out and looked its worst. The most beautiful landscapes reflected in it looked like boiled spinach, and the best people became hideous, or else they were upside down and had no bodies. Their faces were distorted beyond recognition, and if they had even one freckle it appeared to spread all over the nose and mouth. The demon thought this immensely amusing. If a good thought passed through any one's mind, it turned to a grin in the mirror, and this caused real delight to the demon. All the scholars in the demon's school, for he kept a school, reported that a miracle had taken place : now for the first time it had become possible to see what the world and mankind were really like. They ran about all over with the mirror, till at last there was not a country or a person which had not been seen in this distorting mirror. They even wanted to fly up to heaven with it to mock the angels; but the higher they flew, the more it grinned, so much so that they could hardly hold it, and at last it slipped out of their hands and fell to the earth, shivered into hundreds of millions and billions of bits. Even then it did more harm than ever. Some of these bits were not as big as a grain of sand, and these flew about all over the world, getting into people's eyes, and, once in, they stuck there, and distorted everything they looked at, or made them see everything that was amiss. Each tiniest grain of glass kept the same power as that possessed by the whole mirror. Some people even got a bit of the glass into their hearts, and that was terrible, for the heart became like a lump of ice. Some of the fragments were so big that they were used for window panes, but it was not advisable to look at one's friends through these panes. Other bits were made into spectacles, and it was a bad business when people put on these spectacles meaning to

[illegible]

One day he was in a high state of delight because he had invented a mirror with this peculiarity, that every good and pretty thing reflected in it shrank away to almost nothing.

[illegible]

be just. The bad demon laughed till he split his sides; it tickled him to see the mischief he had done. But some of these fragments were still left floating about the world, and you shall hear what happened to them.

SECOND STORY

ABOUT A LITTLE BOY AND A LITTLE GIRL

IN a big town crowded with houses and people, where there is no room for gardens, people have to be content with flowers in pots instead. In one of these towns lived two children who managed to have something bigger than a flower pot for a garden. They were not brother and sister, but they were just as fond of each other as if they had been. Their parents lived opposite each other in two attic rooms. The roof of one house just touched the roof of the next one, with only a rain-water gutter between them. They each had a little dormer window, and one only had to step over the gutter to get from one house to the other. Each of the parents had a large window-box, in which they grew pot herbs and a little rose-tree. There was one in each box, and they both grew splendidly. Then it occurred to the parents to put the boxes across the gutter, from house to house, and they looked just like two banks of flowers. The pea vines hung down over the edges of the boxes, and the roses threw out long creepers which twined round the windows. It was almost like a green triumphal arch. The boxes were high, and the children knew they must not climb up on to them, but they were often allowed to have their little stools out under the rose-trees, and there they had delightful games. Of course in the winter there was an end to these amusements. The windows were often covered with hoar-frost; then they would warm coppers on the stove and stick them on the frozen panes, where they made lovely peep-holes, as round as possible. Then a bright eye would peep through these holes, one from each window. The little boy's name was Kay, and the little girl's Gerda.

In the summer they could reach each other with one bound, but in the winter they had to go down all the stairs in one house and up all the stairs in the other, and outside there were snowdrifts.

'Look! the white bees are swarming,' said the old grandmother.

'Have they a queen bee, too?' asked the little boy, for he knew that there was a queen among the real bees.

'Yes, indeed they have,' said the grandmother. 'She flies where the swarm is thickest. She is biggest of them all, and she never remains on the ground. She always flies up again to the sky. Many a winter's night she flies through the streets and peeps in at the windows, and then the ice freezes on the panes into wonderful patterns like flowers.'

B

Many a winter's night she flies through the streets and peeps in at the windows, and then the ice freezes on the panes into wonderful patterns like flowers.

[illegible]

'Oh yes, we have seen that,' said both children, and then they knew it was true.

'Can the Snow Queen come in here?' asked the little girl.

'Just let her come,' said the boy, 'and I will put her on the stove, where she will melt.'

But the grandmother smoothed his hair and told him more stories.

In the evening when little Kay was at home and half undressed, he crept up on to the chair by the window, and peeped out of the little hole. A few snow-flakes were falling, and one of these, the biggest, remained on the edge of the window-box. It grew bigger and bigger, till it became the figure of a woman, dressed in the finest white gauze, which appeared to be made of millions of starry flakes. She was delicately lovely, but all ice, glittering, dazzling ice. Still she was alive, her eyes shone like two bright stars, but there was no rest or peace in them. She nodded to the window and waved her hand. The little boy was frightened and jumped down off the chair, and then he fancied that a big bird flew past the window.

The next day was bright and frosty, and then came the thaw —and after that the spring. The sun shone, green buds began to appear, the swallows built their nests, and people began to open their windows. The little children began to play in their garden on the roof again. The roses were in splendid bloom that summer;

the little girl had learnt a hymn, and there was something in it about roses, and that made her think of her own. She sang it to the little boy, and then he sang it with her—

'Where roses deck the flowery vale,
There, Infant Jesus, we thee hail!'

The children took each other by the hands, kissed the roses, and rejoiced in God's bright sunshine, and spoke to it as if the Child Jesus were there. What lovely summer days they were, and how delightful it was to sit out under the fresh rose-trees, which seemed never tired of blooming.

Kay and Gerda were looking at a picture book of birds and animals one day—it had just struck five by the church clock—when Kay said, 'Oh, something struck my heart, and I have got something in my eye!'

The little girl put her arms round his neck, he blinked his eye; there was nothing to be seen.

'I believe it is gone,' he said; but it was not gone. It was one of those very grains of glass from the mirror, the magic mirror. You remember that horrid mirror, in which all good and great things reflected in it became small and mean, while the bad things were magnified, and every flaw became very apparent.

Poor Kay! a grain of it had gone straight to his heart, and

would soon turn it to a lump of ice. He did not feel it any more, but it was still there.

'Why do you cry?' he asked; 'it makes you look ugly; there's nothing the matter with me. How horrid!' he suddenly cried; 'there's a worm in that rose, and that one is quite crooked; after all, they are nasty roses, and so are the boxes they are growing in!' He kicked the box and broke off two of the roses.

'What are you doing, Kay?' cried the little girl. When he saw her alarm, he broke off another rose, and then ran in by his own window, and left dear little Gerda alone.

When she next got out the picture book he said it was only fit for babies in long clothes. When his grandmother told them stories he always had a but—, and if he could manage it, he liked to get behind her chair, put on her spectacles and imitate her. He did it very well and people laughed at him. He was soon able to imitate every one in the street; he could make fun of all their peculiarities and failings. 'He will turn out a clever fellow,' said people. But it was all that bit of glass in his heart, that bit of glass in his eye, and it made him tease little Gerda who was so devoted to him. He played quite different games now; he seemed to have grown older. One winter's day, when the snow was falling fast, he brought in a big magnifying glass; he held out the tail of his blue coat, and let the snow flakes fall upon it.

'Now look through the glass, Gerda!' he said; every snowflake was magnified, and looked like a lovely flower, or a sharply pointed star.

'Do you see how cleverly they are made?' said Kay. 'Much more interesting than looking at real flowers. And there is not a single flaw in them; they are perfect, if only they would not melt.'

Shortly after, he appeared in his thick gloves, with his sledge on his back. He shouted right into Gerda's ear, 'I have got leave to drive in the big square where the other boys play!' and away he went.

In the big square the bolder boys used to tie their little sledges to the farm carts and go a long way in this fashion. They had no end of fun over it. Just in the middle of their games a big sledge came along; it was painted white, and the occupant wore a white fur coat and cap. The sledge drove twice round the square, and Kay quickly tied his sledge on behind. Then off they went, faster, and faster, into the next street. The driver turned round and nodded to Kay in the most friendly way, just as if they knew each other. Every time Kay wanted to loose his sledge the person nodded again, and Kay stayed where he was, and they drove right out through the town gates. Then the snow began to fall so heavily that the little boy could not see a hand before him as they rushed along. He undid the cords and tried to get away from the big sledge, but it was no use, his little sledge stuck fast, and on they rushed, faster than the wind. He shouted aloud, but nobody heard him, and the sledge tore on through the snow-drifts. Every now and then it gave a bound, as if they were jumping over hedges and ditches. He was very frightened, and he wanted to say his prayers, but he could only remember the multiplication tables.

The snow-flakes grew bigger and bigger, till at last they looked like big white chickens. All at once they sprang on one side, the big sledge stopped and the person who drove got up, coat and cap smothered in snow. It was a tall and upright lady all shining white, the Snow Queen herself.

'We have come along at a good pace,' she said; 'but it's cold enough to kill one; creep inside my bearskin coat.'

She took him into the sledge by her, wrapped him in her furs, and he felt as if he were sinking into a snowdrift.

'Are you still cold?' she asked, and she kissed him on the forehead. Ugh! it was colder than ice, it went to his very heart, which was already more than half ice; he felt as if he were dying, but only for a moment, and then it seemed to have done him good; he no longer felt the cold.

'My sledge! don't forget my sledge!' He only remembered it now; it was tied to one of the white chickens which flew along behind them. The Snow Queen kissed Kay again, and then he forgot all about little Gerda, Grandmother, and all the others at home.

'Now I mustn't kiss you any more,' she said, 'or I should kiss you to death!'

Kay looked at her, she was so pretty; a cleverer, more beautiful face could hardly be imagined. She did not seem to be made of ice now, as she was outside the window when she waved her hand to him. In his eyes she was quite perfect, and he was not a bit afraid of her; he told her that he could do mental arithmetic, as far as fractions, and that he knew the number of square miles and the number of inhabitants of the country. She always smiled at him, and he then thought that he surely did not know enough, and he looked up into the wide expanse of heaven, into which they rose higher and higher as she flew with him on a dark cloud, while the storm surged around them, the wind ringing in their ears like well-known old songs.

They flew over woods and lakes, over oceans and islands; the cold wind whistled down below them, the wolves howled, the black crows flew screaming over the sparkling snow, but up above, the moon shone bright and clear—and Kay looked at it all the long, long winter nights; in the day he slept at the Snow Queen's feet.

STORY THREE

THE GARDEN OF THE WOMAN LEARNED IN MAGIC

BUT how was little Gerda getting on all this long time since Kay left her? Where could he be? Nobody knew, nobody could say anything about him. All that the other boys knew was, that they had seen him tie his little sledge to a splendid big one which drove away down the street and out of the town gates. Nobody knew where he was, and many tears were shed; little Gerda cried long and bitterly. At last, people said he was dead; he must have fallen into the river which ran close by the town. Oh, what long, dark, winter days those were!

At last the spring came and the sunshine.

'Kay is dead and gone,' said little Gerda.

'I don't believe it,' said the sunshine.

'He is dead and gone,' she said to the swallows.

'We don't believe it,' said the swallows; and at last little Gerda did not believe it either.

'I will put on my new red shoes,' she said one morning; 'those Kay never saw; and then I will go down to the river and ask it about him!'

It was very early in the morning; she kissed the old grandmother, who was still asleep, put on the red shoes, and went quite alone, out by the gate to the river.

'Is it true that you have taken my little playfellow? I will give you my red shoes if you will bring him back to me again.'

She thought the little ripples nodded in such a curious way, so she took off her red shoes, her most cherished possessions, and threw them both into the river. They fell close by the shore, and were carried straight back to her by the little wavelets; it seemed as if the river would not accept her offering, as it had not taken little Kay.

She only thought she had not thrown them far enough; so she climbed into a boat which lay among the rushes, then she went right out to the further end of it, and threw the shoes into the water again. But the boat was loose, and her movements started it off, and it floated away from the shore: she felt it moving and tried to get out, but before she reached the other end the boat was more than a yard from the shore, and was floating away quite quickly.

Little Gerda was terribly frightened, and began to cry, but nobody heard her except the sparrows, and they could not carry her ashore, but they flew alongside twittering, as if to cheer her, 'We are here, we are here.' The boat floated rapidly away with the current; little Gerda sat quite still with only her stockings on; her little red shoes floated behind, but they could not catch up the boat, which drifted away faster and faster.

The banks on both sides were very pretty with beautiful flowers, fine old trees, and slopes dotted with sheep and cattle, but not a single person.

'Perhaps the river is taking me to little Kay,' thought Gerda, and that cheered her; she sat up and looked at the beautiful green banks for hours.

Then they came to a big cherry garden; there was a little

[illegible]

Then an old, old woman came out of the house; she was leaning upon a big, hooked stick, and she wore a big sun hat, which was covered with beautiful painted flowers.

[illegible]

house in it, with curious blue and red windows, it had a thatched roof, and two wooden soldiers stood outside, who presented arms as she sailed past. Gerda called out to them; she thought they were alive, but of course they did not answer; she was quite close to them, for the current drove the boat close to the bank. Gerda called out again, louder than before, and then an old, old woman came out of the house; she was leaning upon a big, hooked stick, and she wore a big sun hat, which was covered with beautiful painted flowers.

'You poor little child,' said the old woman, 'how ever were you driven out on this big, strong river into the wide, wide world alone?' Then she walked right into the water, and caught hold of the boat with her hooked stick; she drew it ashore, and lifted little Gerda out.

Gerda was delighted to be on dry land again, but she was a little bit frightened of the strange old woman.

'Come, tell me who you are, and how you got here,' said she.

When Gerda had told her the whole story and asked her if she had seen Kay, the woman said she had not seen him, but that she expected him. Gerda must not be sad, she was to come and taste her cherries and see her flowers, which were more beautiful than any picture-book; each one had a story to tell. Then she took Gerda by the hand, they went into the little house, and the old woman locked the door.

The windows were very high up, and they were red, blue, and yellow; they threw a very curious light into the room. On the table were quantities of the most delicious cherries, of which Gerda had leave to eat as many as ever she liked. While she was eating, the old woman combed her hair with a golden comb, so that the hair curled, and shone like gold round the pretty little face, which was as sweet as a rose.

'I have long wanted a little girl like you!' said the old woman. 'You will see how well we shall get on together.' While she combed her hair Gerda had forgotten all about Kay, for the old woman was learned in the magic art; but she was not a bad witch, she only cast spells over people for a little amusement, and she wanted to keep Gerda. She therefore went into the garden and waved her hooked stick over all the rose-bushes, and however beautifully they were flowering, all sank down into the rich black earth without leaving a trace behind them. The old woman was afraid that if Gerda saw the roses she would be reminded of Kay, and would want to run away. Then she took Gerda into the flower garden. What a delicious scent there was! and every imaginable flower for every season was in that lovely garden; no picture-book could be brighter or more beautiful. Gerda jumped for joy and played till the sun went down behind the tall cherry trees. Then she was put into a lovely bed with rose-coloured silken coverings stuffed with violets; she slept and dreamt as lovely dreams as any queen on her wedding day.

The next day she played with the flowers in the garden again —and many days passed in the same way. Gerda knew every flower, but however many there were, she always thought there was one missing, but which it was she did not know.

One day she was sitting looking at the old woman's sun hat with its painted flowers, and the very prettiest one of them all was a rose. The old woman had forgotten her hat when she charmed the others away. This is the consequence of being absent-minded.

'What!' said Gerda, 'are there no roses here?' and she sprang in among the flower-beds and sought, but in vain! Her hot tears fell on the very places where the roses used to be; when the warm drops moistened the earth the rose-trees shot up again, just as full of bloom as when they sank. Gerda embraced the roses and kissed them, and then she thought of the lovely roses at home, and this brought the thought of little Kay.

'Oh, how I have been delayed,' said the little girl, 'I ought to have been looking for Kay! Don't you know where he is?' she asked the roses. 'Do you think he is dead and gone?'

'He is not dead,' said the roses. 'For we have been down underground, you know, and all the dead people are there, but Kay is not among them.'

'Oh, thank you!' said little Gerda, and then she went to the other flowers and looked into their cups and said, 'Do you know where Kay is?'

But each flower stood in the sun and dreamt its own dreams. Little Gerda heard many of these, but never anything about Kay.

And what said the Tiger lilies?

'Do you hear the drum? rub-a-dub, it has only two notes, rub-a-dub, always the same. The wailing of women and the cry of the preacher. The Hindu woman in her long red garment stands on the pile, while the flames surround her and her dead husband. But the woman is only thinking of the living man in the circle round, whose eyes burn with a fiercer fire than that of the flames which consume the body. Do the flames of the heart die in the fire?'

'I understand nothing about that,' said little Gerda.

'That is my story,' said the Tiger lily.

'What does the convolvulus say?'

'An old castle is perched high over a narrow mountain path, it is closely covered with ivy, almost hiding the old red walls, and creeping up leaf upon leaf right round the balcony where stands a beautiful maiden. She bends over the balustrade and looks eagerly up the road. No rose on its stem is fresher than she; no apple blossom wafted by the wind moves more lightly. Her silken robes rustle softly as she bends over and says, 'Will he never come?'

'Is it Kay you mean?' asked Gerda.

'I am only talking about my own story, my dream,' answered the convolvulus.

What said the little snowdrop?

'Between two trees a rope with a board is hanging; it is a swing. Two pretty little girls in snowy frocks and green ribbons fluttering on their hats are seated on it. Their brother, who is bigger than they are, stands up behind them; he has his arms round the ropes for supports, and holds in one hand a little bowl and in the other a clay pipe. He is blowing soap-bubbles. As the swing moves the bubbles fly upwards in all their changing colours, the last one still hangs from the pipe swayed by the wind, and the swing goes on. A little black dog runs up, he is almost as light as the bubbles, he stands up on his hind legs and wants to be taken into the swing, but it does not stop. The little dog falls with an angry bark; they jeer at it; the bubble bursts. A swinging plank, a fluttering foam picture—that is my story!'

'I daresay what you tell me is very pretty, but you speak so sadly and you never mention little Kay.'

What says the hyacinth?

'They were three beautiful sisters, all most delicate, and quite transparent. One wore a crimson robe, the other a blue, and the third was pure white. These three danced hand-in-hand, by the edge of the lake in the moonlight. They were human beings, not fairies of the wood. The fragrant air attracted them, and they vanished into the wood; here the fragrance was stronger still. Three coffins glide out of the wood towards the lake, and in them lie the maidens. The fire-flies flutter lightly round them with their little flickering torches. Do these dancing maidens sleep, or are they dead? The scent of the flower says that they are corpses. The evening bell tolls their knell.'

'You make me quite sad,' said little Gerda; 'your perfume is so strong it makes me think of those dead maidens. Oh, is little Kay really dead? The roses have been down underground, and they say no.'

'Ding, dong,' tolled the hyacinth bells; 'we are not tolling for little Kay; we know nothing about him. We sing our song, the only one we know.'

And Gerda went on to the buttercups shining among their dark green leaves.

'You are a bright little sun,' said Gerda. 'Tell me if you know where I shall find my playfellow.'

The buttercup shone brightly and returned Gerda's glance. What song could the buttercup sing? It would not be about Kay.

'God's bright sun shone into a little court on the first day of spring. The sunbeams stole down the neighbouring white wall, close to which bloomed the first yellow flower of the season; it shone like burnished gold in the sun. An old woman had brought her arm-chair out into the sun; her granddaughter, a poor and pretty little maid-servant, had come to pay her a short visit, and she kissed her. There was gold, heart's gold, in the kiss. Gold on the lips, gold on the ground, and gold above, in the early morning beams! Now that is my little story,' said the buttercup.

'Oh, my poor old grandmother!' sighed Gerda. 'She will be longing to see me, and grieving about me, as she did about Kay. But I shall soon go home again and take Kay with me. It is useless for me to ask the flowers about him. They only know their own stories, and have no information to give me.'

Then she tucked up her little dress, so that she might run the faster; but the narcissus blossoms struck her on the legs as she jumped over them, so she stopped and said, 'Perhaps you can tell me something.'

She stooped down close to the flower and listened. What did it say?

'I can see myself, I can see myself,' said the narcissus. 'Oh, how sweet is my scent. Up there in an attic window stands a little dancing girl half dressed; first she stands on one leg, then on the other, and looks as if she would tread the whole world under her feet. She is only a delusion. She pours some water out of a teapot on to a bit of stuff that she is holding; it is her bodice. "Cleanliness is a good thing," she says. Her white dress hangs on a peg; it has been washed in the teapot, too, and dried on the roof. She puts it on, and wraps a saffron-coloured scarf round her neck, which makes the dress look whiter. See how high she carries her head, and all upon one stem. I see myself, I see myself!'

'I don't care a bit about all that,' said Gerda; 'it's no use telling me such stuff.'

And then she ran to the end of the garden. The door was fastened, but she pressed the rusty latch, and it gave way. The door sprang open, and little Gerda ran out with bare feet into the wide world. She looked back three times, but nobody came after her. At last she could run no further, and she sat down on a big stone. When she looked round she saw that the summer was over; it was quite late autumn. She would never have known it inside the beautiful garden, where the sun always shone, and the flowers of every season were always in bloom.

'Oh, how I have wasted my time,' said little Gerda. 'It is autumn. I must not rest any longer,' and she got up to go on.

Oh, how weary and sore were her little feet, and everything round looked so cold and dreary. The long willow leaves were quite yellow. The damp mist fell off the trees like rain, one leaf dropped after another from the trees, and only the sloe-thorn still bore its fruit; but the sloes were sour and set one's teeth on edge. Oh, how grey and sad it looked, out in the wide world.

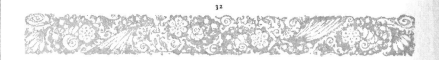

FOURTH STORY

PRINCE AND PRINCESS

GERDA was soon obliged to rest again. A big crow hopped on to the snow, just in front of her. It had been sitting looking at her for a long time and wagging its head. Now it said, 'Caw, caw ; good-day, good-day,' as well as it could ; it meant to be kind to the little girl, and asked her where she was going, alone in the wide world.

Gerda understood the word 'alone' and knew how much there was in it, and she told the crow the whole story of her life and adventures, and asked if it had seen Kay.

The crow nodded its head gravely and said, 'May be I have, may be I have.'

'What, do you really think you have?' cried the little girl, nearly smothering him with her kisses.

'Gently, gently!' said the crow. 'I believe it may have been Kay, but he has forgotten you by this time, I expect, for the Princess.'

'Does he live with a Princess?' asked Gerda.

'Yes, listen,' said the crow; 'but it is so difficult to speak your language. If you understand "crow's language,"[1] I can tell you about it much better.'

'No, I have never learnt it,' said Gerda; 'but grandmother knew it, and used to speak it. If only I had learnt it!'

'It doesn't matter,' said the crow. 'I will tell you as well as I can, although I may do it rather badly.'

Then he told her what he had heard.

'In this kingdom where we are now,' said he, 'there lives a Princess who is very clever. She has read all the newspapers in the world, and forgotten them again, so clever is she. One day she was sitting on her throne, which is not such an amusing thing to do either, they say; and she began humming a tune, which happened to be

"Why should I not be married, oh why?"

"Why not indeed?" said she. And she made up her mind to marry, if she could find a husband who had an answer ready when a question was put to him. She called all the court ladies together, and when they heard what she wanted they were delighted.

'"I like that now," they said. "I was thinking the same thing myself the other day."

[1] Children have a kind of language, or gibberish, formed by adding letters or syllables to every word, which is called 'crow's language.'

[illegible]

She has read all the newspapers in the world, and forgotten them again, so clever is she.

[illegible]

'Every word I say is true,' said the crow, 'for I have a tame sweetheart who goes about the palace whenever she likes. She told me the whole story.'

Of course his sweetheart was a crow, for 'birds of a feather flock together,' and one crow always chooses another. The newspapers all came out immediately with borders of hearts and the Princess's initials. They gave notice that any young man who was handsome enough might go up to the Palace to speak to the Princess. The one who spoke as if he were quite at home, and spoke well, would be chosen by the Princess as her husband. Yes, yes, you may believe me, it's as true as I sit here,' said the crow. 'The people came crowding in; there was such running, and crushing, but no one was fortunate enough to be chosen, either on the first day, or on the second. They could all of them talk well enough in the street, but when they entered the castle gates, and saw the guard in silver uniforms, and when they went up the stairs through rows of lackeys in gold embroidered liveries, their courage forsook them. When they reached the brilliantly lighted reception-rooms, and stood in front of the throne where the Princess was seated, they could think of nothing to say, they only echoed her last words, and of course that was not what she wanted.

'It was just as if they had all taken some kind of sleeping-powder, which made them lethargic; they did not recover themselves until they got out into the street again, and then they had plenty to say. There was quite a long line of them, reaching from the town gates up to the Palace.

'I went to see them myself,' said the crow. 'They were hungry and thirsty, but they got nothing at the Palace, not even as much as a glass of tepid water. Some of the wise ones had taken sandwiches with them, but they did not share them with their neighbours; they thought if the others went in to the Princess looking hungry, that there would be more chance for themselves.'

'But Kay, little Kay!' asked Gerda; 'when did he come? was he amongst the crowd?'

'Give me time, give me time! we are just coming to him. It was on the third day that a little personage came marching cheerfully along, without either carriage or horse. His eyes sparkled like yours, and he had beautiful long hair, but his clothes were very shabby.'

'Oh, that was Kay!' said Gerda gleefully; 'then I have found him!' and she clapped her hands.

'He had a little knapsack on his back!' said the crow.

'No, it must have been his sledge; he had it with him when he went away!' said Gerda.

'It may be so,' said the crow; 'I did not look very particularly; but I know from my sweetheart, that when he entered the Palace gates, and saw the life-guards in their silver uniforms, and the lackeys on the stairs in their gold-laced liveries, he was not the least bit abashed. He just nodded to them and said, "It must be very tiresome to stand upon the stairs. I am going inside!" The rooms were blazing with lights. Privy councillors and excellencies without number were walking about barefoot carrying golden vessels; it was enough to make you solemn! His boots creaked fearfully too, but he wasn't a bit upset.'

'Oh, I am sure that was Kay!' said Gerda; 'I know he had a pair of new boots, I heard them creaking in grandmother's room.'

'Yes, indeed they did creak!' said the crow. 'But nothing daunted, he went straight up to the Princess, who was sitting on a pearl as big as a spinning-wheel. Poor, simple boy! all the court ladies and their attendants; the courtiers, and their gentlemen, each attended by a page, were standing round. The nearer the door they stood, so much the greater was their haughtiness; till the footman's boy, who always wore slippers and stood in the doorway, was almost too proud even to be looked at.'

'It must be awful!' said little Gerda, 'and yet Kay has won the Princess!'

'If I had not been a crow, I should have taken her myself, notwithstanding that I am engaged. They say he spoke as well as I could have done myself, when I speak crow-language; at least so my sweetheart says. He was a picture of good looks and gallantry, and then, he had not come with any idea of wooing the Princess, but simply to hear her wisdom. He admired her just as much as she admired him!'

'Indeed it was Kay then,' said Gerda; 'he was so clever he could do mental arithmetic up to fractions. Oh, won't you take me to the Palace?'

'It's easy enough to talk,' said the crow; 'but how are we to manage it? I will talk to my tame sweetheart about it; she will have some advice to give us I daresay, but I am bound to tell you that a little girl like you will never be admitted!'

'Oh, indeed I shall,' said Gerda; 'when Kay hears that I am here, he will come out at once to fetch me.'

'Wait here for me by the stile,' said the crow, then he wagged his head and flew off.

The evening had darkened in before he came back. 'Caw, caw,' he said, 'she sends you greeting. And here is a little roll for you; she got it out of the kitchen where there is bread enough, and I daresay you are hungry! It is not possible for you to get into the Palace; you have bare feet; the guards in silver and the lackeys in gold would never allow you to pass. But don't cry, we shall get you in somehow; my sweetheart knows a little back staircase which leads up to the bedroom, and she knows where the key is kept.'

Then they went into the garden, into the great avenue where the leaves were dropping, softly one by one; and when the Palace lights went out, one after the other, the crow led little Gerda to the back door, which was ajar.

Oh, how Gerda's heart beat with fear and longing! It was just as if she was about to do something wrong, and yet she only wanted to know if this really was little Kay. Oh, it must be him, she thought, picturing to herself his clever eyes and his long hair. She could see his very smile when they used to sit under the rose-trees at home. She thought he would be very glad to see her, and to hear what a long way she had come to find him, and to hear how sad they had all been at home when he did not come back. Oh, it was joy mingled with fear.

They had now reached the stairs, where a little lamp was burning on a shelf. There stood the tame sweetheart, twisting and turning her head to look at Gerda, who made a curtsy, as grandmother had taught her.

'My betrothed has spoken so charmingly to me about you, my little miss!' she said; 'your life, "*Vita*," as it is called, is most touching! If you will take the lamp, I will go on in front. We shall take the straight road here, and we shall meet no one.'

'It seems to me that some one is coming behind us,' said Gerda, as she fancied something rushed past her, throwing a shadow on the walls; horses with flowing manes and slender legs; huntsmen, ladies and gentlemen on horseback.

'Oh, those are only the dreams!' said the crow; 'they come to take the thoughts of the noble ladies and gentlemen out hunting. That's a good thing, for you will be able to see them all the better in bed. But don't forget, when you are taken into favour, to show a grateful spirit.'

'Now, there's no need to talk about that,' said the crow from the woods.

They came now into the first apartment; it was hung with rose-coloured satin embroidered with flowers. Here again the dreams overtook them, but they flitted by so quickly that Gerda could not distinguish them. The apartments became one more beautiful than the other; they were enough to bewilder anybody. They now reached the bedroom. The ceiling was like a great palm with crystal leaves, and in the middle of the room two beds, each like a lily hung from a golden stem. One was white, and in it lay the Princess; the other was red, and there lay he whom Gerda had come to seek—little Kay! She bent aside one of the crimson leaves, and she saw a little brown neck. It was Kay. She called his name aloud, and held the lamp close to him. Again the dreams rushed through the room on horseback—he awoke, turned his head—and it was not little Kay.

It was only the Prince's neck which was like his; but he was young and handsome. The Princess peeped out of her lily-white bed, and asked what was the matter. Then little Gerda cried and told them all her story, and what the crows had done to help her.

'You poor little thing!' said the Prince and Princess. And they praised the crows, and said that they were not at all angry with them, but they must not do it again. Then they gave them a reward.

'Would you like your liberty?' said the Princess, 'or would you prefer permanent posts about the court as court crows, with perquisites from the kitchen?'

Both crows curtsied and begged for the permanent posts, for they thought of their old age, and said 'it was so good to have something for the old man,' as they called it.

The Prince got up and allowed Gerda to sleep in his bed, and he could not have done more. She folded her little hands, and thought 'how good the people and the animals are'; then she shut her eyes and fell fast asleep. All the dreams came flying back again; this time they looked like angels, and they were dragging a little sledge with Kay sitting on it, and he nodded. But it was only a dream; so it all vanished when she woke.

Next day she was dressed in silk and velvet from head to foot; they asked her to stay at the Palace and have a good time, but she only begged them to give her a little carriage and horse, and a little pair of boots, so that she might drive out into the wide world to look for Kay.

They gave her a pair of boots and a muff. She was beautifully dressed, and when she was ready to start, there before the door stood a new chariot of pure gold. The Prince's and Princess's coat of arms were emblazoned on it, and shone like a star. Coachman, footman, and outrider, for there was even an outrider, all wore golden crowns. The Prince and Princess themselves helped her into the carriage and wished her joy. The wood crow, who was now married, accompanied her for the first three miles; he sat beside Gerda, for he could not ride with his back to the horses. The other crow stood at the door and flapped her wings; she did not go with them, for she suffered from headache since she had become a kitchen pensioner—the consequence of eating too much. The chariot was stored with sugar biscuits, and there were fruit and ginger nuts under the seat. 'Good-bye, good-bye,' cried the Prince and Princess; little Gerda wept, and the crow wept too. At the end of the first few miles the crow said good-bye, and this was the hardest parting of all. It flew up into a tree and flapped its big black wings as long as it could see the chariot, which shone like the brightest sunshine.

FIFTH STORY

THE LITTLE ROBBER GIRL

THEY drove on through a dark wood, where the chariot lighted up the way and blinded the robbers by its glare; it was more than they could bear.

'It is gold, it is gold!' they cried, and darting forward, seized the horses, and killed the postilions, the coachman, and footman. They then dragged little Gerda out of the carriage.

'She is fat, and she is pretty; she has been fattened on nuts!' said the old robber woman, who had a long beard, and eyebrows that hung down over her eyes. 'She is as good as a fat lamb, and how nice she will taste!' She drew out her sharp knife as she said this; it glittered horribly. 'Oh!' screamed the old woman at the same moment, for her little daughter had come up behind her, and she was biting her ear. She hung on her back, as wild and as savage a little animal as you could wish to find. 'You bad, wicked child!' said her mother, but she was prevented from killing Gerda on this occasion.

'She shall play with me,' said the little robber girl; 'she shall give me her muff, and her pretty dress, and she shall sleep in my bed.' Then she bit her mother again and made her dance. All the robbers laughed and said, 'Look at her dancing with her cub!'

'I want to get into the carriage,' said the little robber girl, and she always had her own way because she was so spoilt and stubborn. She and Gerda got into the carriage, and then they drove over stubble and stones further and further into the wood. The little robber girl was as big as Gerda, but much stronger; she had broader shoulders, and darker skin, her eyes were quite black, with almost a melancholy expression. She put her arm round Gerda's waist and said—

'They shan't kill you as long as I don't get angry with you; you must surely be a Princess!'

'No,' said little Gerda, and then she told her all her adventures, and how fond she was of Kay.

The robber girl looked earnestly at her, gave a little nod, and said, 'They shan't kill you even if I am angry with you. I will do it myself.' Then she dried Gerda's eyes, and stuck her own hands into the pretty muff, which was so soft and warm.

At last the chariot stopped: they were in the courtyard of a robber's castle, the walls of which were cracked from top to bottom. Ravens and crows flew in and out of every hole, and big bulldogs, which each looked ready to devour somebody, jumped about as high as they could, but they did not bark, for it

G

'It is gold, it is gold!' they cried.

was not allowed. A big fire was burning in the middle of the stone floor of the smoky old hall. The smoke all went up to the ceiling, where it had to find a way out for itself. Soup was boiling in a big caldron over the fire, and hares and rabbits were roasting on the spits.

'You shall sleep with me and all my little pets to-night,' said the robber girl.

When they had something to eat and drink they went along to one corner which was spread with straw and rugs. There were nearly a hundred pigeons roosting overhead on the rafters and beams. They seemed to be asleep, but they fluttered about a little when the children came in.

'They are all mine,' said the little robber girl, seizing one of the nearest. She held it by the legs and shook it till it flapped its wings. 'Kiss it,' she cried, dashing it at Gerda's face. 'Those are the wood pigeons,' she added, pointing to some laths fixed across a big hole high up on the walls; 'they are a regular rabble; they would fly away directly if they were not locked in. And here is my old sweetheart Be,' dragging forward a reindeer by the horn; it was tied up, and it had a bright copper ring round its neck. 'We have to keep him close too, or he would run off. Every single night I tickle his neck with my bright knife, he is so frightened of it.' The little girl produced a long knife out of a hole in the wall and drew it across the reindeer's neck. The poor animal laughed and kicked, and the robber girl laughed and pulled Gerda down into the bed with her.

'Do you have that knife by you while you are asleep?' asked Gerda, looking rather frightened.

'I always sleep with a knife,' said the little robber girl. 'You never know what will happen. But now tell me again what you told me before about little Kay, and why you went out into the world.' So Gerda told her all about it again, and the wood pigeons cooed up in their cage above them; the other pigeons were asleep. The little robber girl put her arm round Gerda's neck and went to sleep with the knife in her other hand, and she was soon snoring. But Gerda would not close her eyes; she did not know whether she was to live or to die. The robbers sat round the fire, eating and drinking, and the old woman was turning somersaults. This sight terrified the poor little girl. Then the wood pigeons said, 'Coo, coo, we have seen little Kay; his sledge was drawn by a white chicken, and he was sitting in the Snow Queen's sledge; it was floating low down over the trees, while we were in our nests. She blew upon us young ones, and they all died except we two; coo, coo.'

'What are you saying up there?' asked Gerda. 'Where was the Snow Queen going? Do you know anything about it?'

'She was most likely going to Lapland, because there is

always snow and ice there! Ask the reindeer who is tied up there.'

'There is ice and snow, and it's a splendid place,' said the reindeer. 'You can run and jump about where you like on those big glittering plains. The Snow Queen has her summer tent there, but her permanent castle is up at the North Pole, on the island which is called Spitzbergen!'

'Oh Kay, little Kay!' sighed Gerda.

'Lie still, or I shall stick the knife into you!' said the robber girl.

In the morning Gerda told her all that the wood pigeons had said, and the little robber girl looked quite solemn, but she nodded her head and said, 'No matter, no matter! Do you know where Lapland is?' she asked the reindeer.

'Who should know better than I,' said the animal, its eyes dancing. 'I was born and brought up there, and I used to leap about on the snowfields.'

'Listen,' said the robber girl. 'You see that all our men folks are away, but mother is still here, and she will stay; but later on in the morning she will take a drink out of the big bottle there, and after that she will have a nap—then I will do something for you.' Then she jumped out of bed, ran along to her mother and pulled her beard, and said, 'Good morning, my own dear nanny-goat!' And her mother filliped her nose till it was red and blue; but it was all affection.

As soon as her mother had had her draught from the bottle and had dropped asleep, the little robber girl went along to the reindeer, and said, 'I should have the greatest pleasure in the world in keeping you here, to tickle you with my knife, because you are such fun then; however, it does not matter. I will untie your halter and help you outside so that you may run away to Lapland, but you must put your best foot foremost, and take this little girl for me to the Snow Queen's palace, where her playfellow is. I have no doubt you heard what she was telling me, for she spoke loud enough, and you are generally eavesdropping!'

The reindeer jumped into the air for joy. The robber girl lifted little Gerda up, and had the forethought to tie her on, nay, even to give her a little cushion to sit upon. 'Here, after all, I will give you your fur boots back, for it will be very cold, but I will keep your muff, it is too pretty to part with. Still you shan't be cold. Here are my mother's big mittens for you, they will reach up to your elbows; here, stick your hands in! Now your hands look just like my nasty mother's!'

Gerda shed tears of joy.

'I don't like you to whimper!' said the little robber girl. 'You ought to be looking delighted; and here are two loaves and a ham for you, so that you shan't starve.'

These things were tied on to the back of the reindeer; the little robber girl opened the door, called in all the big dogs, and then she cut the halter with her knife, and said to the reindeer, 'Now run, but take care of my little girl!'

Gerda stretched out her hands in the big mittens to the robber girl and said good-bye; and then the reindeer darted off over briars and bushes, through the big wood, over swamps and plains, as fast as it could go. The wolves howled and the ravens screamed, while the red lights quivered up in the sky.

'There are my old northern lights,' said the reindeer; 'see how they flash!' and on it rushed faster than ever, day and night. The loaves were eaten, and the ham too, and then they were in Lapland.

SIXTH STORY

THE LAPP WOMAN AND THE FINN WOMAN

THEY stopped by a little hut, a very poverty-stricken one; the roof sloped right down to the ground, and the door was so low that the people had to creep on hands and knees when they wanted to go in or out. There was nobody at home here but an old Lapp woman, who was frying fish over a train-oil lamp. The reindeer told her all Gerda's story, but it told its own first; for it thought it was much the most important. Gerda was so overcome by the cold that she could not speak at all.

'Oh, you poor creatures!' said the Lapp woman; 'you've got a long way to go yet; you will have to go hundreds of miles into Finmark, for the Snow Queen is paying a country visit there, and she burns blue lights every night. I will write a few words on a dried stock-fish, for I have no paper. I will give it to you to take to the Finn woman up there. She will be better able to direct you than I can.'

So when Gerda was warmed, and had eaten and drunk something, the Lapp woman wrote a few words on a dried stock-fish and gave it to her, bidding her take good care of it. Then she tied her on to the reindeer again, and off they flew. Flicker, flicker, went the beautiful blue northern lights up in the sky all night long;—at last they came to Finmark, and knocked on the Finn woman's chimney, for she had no door at all.

There was such a heat inside that the Finn woman went about almost naked; she was little and very grubby. She at once loosened Gerda's things, and took off the mittens and the boots, or she would have been too hot. Then she put a piece of ice on the reindeer's head, and after that she read what was written on the stock-fish. She read it three times, and then she knew it by heart, and put the fish into the pot for dinner; there was no reason why it should not be eaten, and she never wasted anything.

Again the reindeer told his own story first, and then little

Gerda's. The Finn woman blinked with her wise eyes, but she said nothing.

'You are so clever,' said the reindeer, 'I know you can bind all the winds of the world with a bit of sewing cotton. When a skipper unties one knot he gets a good wind, when he unties two it blows hard, and if he undoes the third and the fourth he brings a storm about his head wild enough to blow down the forest trees. Won't you give the little girl a drink, so that she may have the strength of twelve men to overcome the Snow Queen?'

'The strength of twelve men,' said the Finn woman. 'Yes, that will be about enough.'

She went along to a shelf and took down a big folded skin, which she unrolled. There were curious characters written on it, and the Finn woman read till the perspiration poured down her forehead.

But the reindeer again implored her to give Gerda something, and Gerda looked at her with such beseeching eyes, full of tears, that the Finn woman began blinking again, and drew the reindeer along into a corner, where she whispered to it, at the same time putting fresh ice on its head.

'Little Kay is certainly with the Snow Queen, and he is delighted with everything there. He thinks it is the best place in the world, but that is because he has got a splinter of glass in his heart and a grain of glass in his eye. They will have to come out first, or he will never be human again, and the Snow Queen will keep him in her power!'

'But can't you give little Gerda something to take which will give her power to conquer it all?'

'I can't give her greater power than she already has. Don't you see how great it is? Don't you see how both man and beast have to serve her? How she has got on as well as she has on her bare feet? We must not tell her what power she has; it is in her heart, because she is such a sweet innocent child. If she can't reach the Snow Queen herself, then we can't help her. The Snow Queen's gardens begin just two miles from here; you can carry the little girl as far as that. Put her down by the big bush standing there in the snow covered with red berries. Don't stand gossiping, but hurry back to me!' Then the Finn woman lifted Gerda on the reindeer's back, and it rushed off as hard as it could.

'Oh, I have not got my boots, and I have not got my mittens!' cried little Gerda.

She soon felt the want of them in that cutting wind, but the reindeer did not dare to stop. It ran on till it came to the bush with the red berries. There it put Gerda down, and kissed her on the mouth, while big shining tears trickled down its face. Then it ran back again as fast as ever it could. There stood poor little

[illegible]

The reindeer did not dare to stop. It ran on till it came to the bush with the red berries. There it put Gerda down, and kissed her on the mouth, while big shining tears trickled down its face.

Gerda, without shoes or gloves, in the middle of freezing icebound Finmark.

She ran forward as quickly as she could. A whole regiment of snow-flakes came towards her; they did not fall from the sky, for it was quite clear, with the northern lights shining brightly. No; these snow-flakes ran along the ground, and the nearer they came the bigger they grew. Gerda remembered well how big and ingenious they looked under the magnifying glass. But the size of these was monstrous. They were alive; they were the Snow Queen's advanced guard, and they took the most curious shapes. Some looked like big, horrid porcupines, some like bundles of knotted snakes with their heads sticking out. Others, again, were like fat little bears with bristling hair, but all were dazzling white and living snow-flakes.

Then little Gerda said the Lord's Prayer, and the cold was so great that her breath froze as it came out of her mouth, and she could see it like a cloud of smoke in front of her. It grew thicker and thicker, till it formed itself into bright little angels, who grew bigger and bigger when they touched the ground. They all wore helmets, and carried shields and spears in their hands. More and more of them appeared, and when Gerda had finished her prayer she was surrounded by a whole legion. They pierced the snow-flakes with their spears and shivered them into a hundred pieces, and little Gerda walked fearlessly and undauntedly through them.

The angels touched her hands and her feet, and then she hardly felt how cold it was, but walked quickly on towards the Palace of the Snow Queen.

Now we must see what Kay was about. He was not thinking about Gerda at all, least of all that she was just outside the Palace.

SEVENTH STORY

WHAT HAPPENED IN THE SNOW QUEEN'S PALACE AND AFTERWARDS

THE Palace walls were made of drifted snow, and the windows and doors of the biting winds. There were over a hundred rooms in it, shaped just as the snow had drifted. The biggest one stretched for many miles. They were all lighted by the strongest northern lights. All the rooms were immensely big and empty, and glittering in their iciness. There was never any gaiety in them; not even so much as a ball for the little bears, when the storms might have turned up as the orchestra, and the polar bears might have walked about on their hind legs and shown off their grand manners. There was never even a little game-playing party, for such games as 'touch last' or 'the biter bit'—no, not even a little gossip over the coffee cups for the white fox misses. Immense, vast, and cold were the Snow Queen's halls. The northern lights came and went with such regularity that you could count the seconds between their coming and going. In the midst of these never-ending snow-halls was a frozen lake. It was broken up on the surface into a thousand bits, but each piece was so exactly like the others that the whole formed a perfect work of art. The Snow Queen sat in the very middle of it when she sat at home. She then said that she was sitting on 'The Mirror of Reason,' and that it was the best and only one in the world.

Little Kay was blue with cold, nay, almost black ; but he did not know it, for the Snow Queen had kissed away the icy shiverings, and his heart was little better than a lump of ice. He went about dragging some sharp, flat pieces of ice, which he placed in all sorts of patterns, trying to make something out of them ; just as when we at home have little tablets of wood, with which we make patterns, and call them a 'Chinese puzzle.'

Kay's patterns were most ingenious, because they were the 'Ice Puzzles of Reason.' In his eyes they were first-rate and of the greatest importance : this was because of the grain of glass still in his eye. He made many patterns forming words, but he never could find out the right way to place them for one particular word, a word he was most anxious to make. It was 'Eternity.' The Snow Queen had said to him that if he could find out this word he should be his own master, and she would give him the whole world and a new pair of skates. But he could not discover it.

'Now I am going to fly away to the warm countries,' said the Snow Queen. 'I want to go and peep into the black caldrons!' She meant the volcanoes Etna and Vesuvius by this. 'I must whiten them a little; it does them good, and the lemons and the grapes too!' And away she flew.

Kay sat quite alone in all those many miles of empty ice halls. He looked at his bits of ice, and thought and thought, till something gave way within him. He sat so stiff and immovable that one might have thought he was frozen to death.

Then it was that little Gerda walked into the Palace, through the great gates in a biting wind. She said her evening prayer, and the wind dropped as if lulled to sleep, and she walked on into the big empty hall. She saw Kay, and knew him at once; she flung her arms round his neck, held him fast, and cried, 'Kay, little Kay, have I found you at last?'

But he sat still, rigid and cold.

Then little Gerda shed hot tears; they fell upon his breast and penetrated to his heart. Here they thawed the lump of ice, and melted the little bit of the mirror which was in it. He looked at her, and she sang:

'Where roses deck the flowery vale,
There, Infant Jesus, we thee hail!'

[illegible]

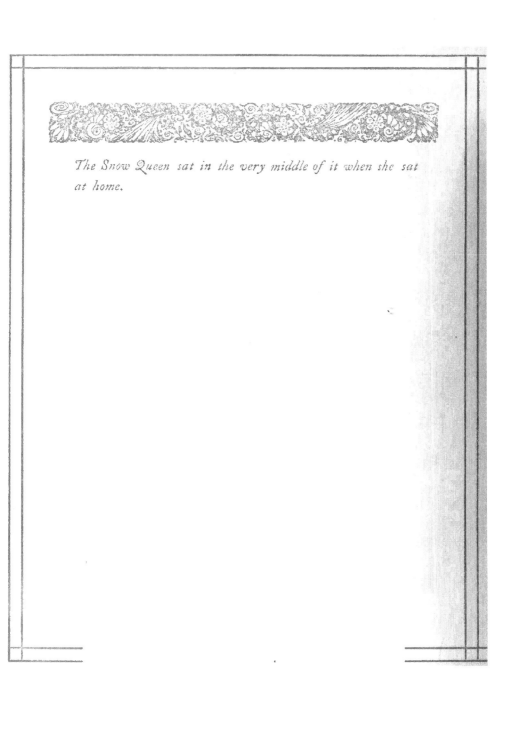

The Snow Queen sat in the very middle of it when she sat at home.

[illegible]

Then Kay burst into tears; he cried so much that the grain of glass was washed out of his eye. He knew her, and shouted with joy, 'Gerda, dear little Gerda! where have you been for such a long time? And where have I been?' He looked round and said, 'How cold it is here; how empty and vast!' He kept tight hold of Gerda, who laughed and cried for joy. Their happiness was so heavenly that even the bits of ice danced for joy around them; and when they settled down, there they lay! just in the very position the Snow Queen had told Kay he must find out, if he was to become his own master and have the whole world and a new pair of skates.

Gerda kissed his cheeks and they grew rosy, she kissed his eyes and they shone like hers, she kissed his hands and his feet, and he became well and strong. The Snow Queen might come home whenever she liked, his order of release was written there in shining letters of ice.

They took hold of each other's hands and wandered out of the big Palace. They talked about grandmother, and about the roses upon the roof. Wherever they went the winds lay still and the sun broke through the clouds. When they reached the bush with the red berries they found the reindeer waiting for them, and he had brought another young reindeer with him, whose udders were full. The children drank her warm milk and kissed her on the mouth. Then they carried Kay and Gerda, first to the Finn woman, in whose heated hut they warmed themselves and received directions about the homeward journey. Then they went on to the Lapp woman; she had made new clothes for them and prepared her sledge. Both the reindeer ran by their side, to the boundaries of the country; here the first green buds appeared, and they said 'Good-bye' to the reindeer and the Lapp woman. They heard the first little birds twittering and saw the buds in the forest. Out of it came riding a young girl on a beautiful horse, which Gerda knew, for it had drawn the golden chariot. She had a scarlet cap on her head and pistols in her belt; it was the little robber girl, who was tired of being at home. She was riding northwards to see how she liked it before she tried some other part of the world. She knew them again, and Gerda recognised her with delight.

'You are a nice fellow to go tramping off!' she said to little Kay. 'I should like to know if you deserve to have somebody running to the end of the world for your sake!'

But Gerda patted her cheek, and asked about the Prince and Princess.

'They are travelling in foreign countries,' said the robber girl.

'But the crow?' asked Gerda.

'Oh, the crow is dead!' she answered. 'The tame sweetheart is a widow, and goes about with a bit of black wool tied round her leg. She pities herself bitterly, but it 's all nonsense! But tell me how you got on yourself, and where you found him.'

Gerda and Kay both told her all about it.

'Snip, snap, snurre, it 's all right at last then!' she said, and she took hold of their hands and promised that if she ever passed through their town she would pay them a visit. Then she rode off into the wide world. But Kay and Gerda walked on, hand in hand, and wherever they went they found the most delightful spring and blooming flowers. Soon they recognised the big town where they lived, with its tall towers, in which the bells still rang their merry peals. They went straight on to grandmother's door, up the stairs and into her room. Everything was just as they had left it, and the old clock ticked in the corner, and the hands pointed to the time. As they went through the door into the room they perceived that they were grown up. The roses clustered round the open window, and there stood their two little chairs. Kay and Gerda sat down upon them, still holding each other by the hand. All the cold empty grandeur of the Snow Queen's palace had passed from their memory like a bad dream. Grandmother sat in God's warm sunshine reading from her Bible.

'Without ye become as little children ye cannot enter into the Kingdom of Heaven.'

Kay and Gerda looked into each other's eyes, and then all at once the meaning of the old hymn came to them.

> ' Where roses deck the flowery vale,
> There, Infant Jesus, we thee hail !'

And there they both sat, grown up and yet children, children at heart ; and it was summer—warm, beautiful summer.

THE NIGHTINGALE

IN China, as you know, the Emperor is a Chinaman, and all the people around him are Chinamen too. It is many years since the story I am going to tell you happened, but that is all the more reason for telling it, lest it should be forgotten. The emperor's palace was the most beautiful thing in the world ; it was made entirely of the finest porcelain, very costly, but at the same time so fragile that it could only be touched with the very greatest care. There were the most extraordinary flowers to be seen in the garden ; the most beautiful ones had little silver bells tied to them, which tinkled perpetually, so that one should not pass the flowers without looking at them. Every little detail in the garden had been most carefully thought out, and it was so big, that even the gardener himself did not know where it ended. If one went on walking, one came to beautiful woods with lofty trees and deep lakes. The wood extended to the sea, which was deep and blue, deep enough for large ships to sail up right under the branches of the trees. Among these trees lived a nightingale, which sang so deliciously, that even the poor fisherman, who had plenty of other things to do, lay still to listen to it, when he was out at night drawing in his nets. 'Heavens, how beautiful it is!' he said, but then he had to attend to his business and forgot it. The next night when he heard it again he would again exclaim, 'Heavens, how beautiful it is!'

Travellers came to the emperor's capital, from every country in the world; they admired everything very much, especially the palace and the gardens, but when they heard the nightingale they all said, 'This is better than anything!'

When they got home they described it, and the learned ones wrote many books about the town, the palace and the garden; but nobody forgot the nightingale, it was always put above everything else. Those among them who were poets wrote the most beautiful poems, all about the nightingale in the woods by the deep blue sea. These books went all over the world, and in course of time some of them reached the emperor. He sat in his golden chair reading and reading, and nodding his head, well pleased to hear such beautiful descriptions of the town, the palace and the garden. 'But the nightingale is the best of all,' he read.

'What is this?' said the emperor. 'The nightingale? Why, I know nothing about it. Is there such a bird in my kingdom, and in my own garden into the bargain, and I have never

[illegible]

[illegible]

heard of it? Imagine my having to discover this from a book?'

Then he called his gentleman-in-waiting, who was so grand that when any one of a lower rank dared to speak to him, or to ask him a question, he would only answer 'P,' which means nothing at all.

'There is said to be a very wonderful bird called a nightingale here,' said the emperor. 'They say that it is better than anything else in all my great kingdom! Why have I never been told anything about it?'

'I have never heard it mentioned,' said the gentleman-in-waiting. 'It has never been presented at court.'

'I wish it to appear here this evening to sing to me,' said the emperor. 'The whole world knows what I am possessed of, and I know nothing about it!'

'I have never heard it mentioned before,' said the gentleman-in-waiting. 'I will seek it, and I will find it!' But where was it to be found? The gentleman-in-waiting ran upstairs and downstairs and in and out of all the rooms and corridors. No one of all those he met had ever heard anything about the nightingale; so the gentleman-in-waiting ran back to the emperor, and said that it must be a myth, invented by the writers of the books. 'Your imperial majesty must not believe everything that is written; books are often mere inventions, even if they do not belong to what we call the black art!'

'But the book in which I read it is sent to me by the powerful Emperor of Japan, so it can't be untrue. I will hear this nightingale; I insist upon its being here to-night. I extend my most gracious protection to it, and if it is not forthcoming, I will have the whole court trampled upon after supper!'

'Tsing-pe!' said the gentleman-in-waiting, and away he ran again, up and down all the stairs, in and out of all the rooms and corridors; half the court ran with him, for they none of them wished to be trampled on. There was much questioning about this nightingale, which was known to all the outside world, but to no one at court. At last they found a poor little maid in the kitchen. She said, 'Oh heavens, the nightingale? I know it very well. Yes, indeed it can sing. Every evening I am allowed to take broken meat to my poor sick mother: she lives down by the shore. On my way back, when I am tired, I rest awhile in the wood, and then I hear the nightingale. Its song brings the tears into my eyes; I feel as if my mother were kissing me!'

'Little kitchen-maid,' said the gentleman-in-waiting, 'I will procure you a permanent position in the kitchen, and permission to see the emperor dining, if you will take us to the nightingale. It is commanded to appear at court to-night.'

Then they all went out into the wood where the nightingale usually sang. Half the court was there. As they were going along at their best pace a cow began to bellow.

'Oh!' said a young courtier, 'there we have it. What wonderful power for such a little creature; I have certainly heard it before.'

'No, those are the cows bellowing; we are a long way yet from the place.' Then the frogs began to croak in the marsh.

'Beautiful!' said the Chinese chaplain, 'it is just like the tinkling of church bells.'

'No, those are the frogs!' said the little kitchen-maid. 'But I think we shall soon hear it now!'

Then the nightingale began to sing.

'There it is!' said the little girl. 'Listen, listen, there it sits!' and she pointed to a little grey bird up among the branches.

'Is it possible?' said the gentleman-in-waiting. 'I should never have thought it was like that. How common it looks! Seeing so many grand people must have frightened all its colours away.'

'Little nightingale!' called the kitchen-maid quite loud, 'our gracious emperor wishes you to sing to him!'

'With the greatest of pleasure!' said the nightingale, warbling away in the most delightful fashion.

'It is just like crystal bells,' said the gentleman-in-waiting. 'Look at its little throat, how active it is. It is extraordinary that we have never heard it before! I am sure it will be a great success at court!'

'Shall I sing again to the emperor?' said the nightingale, who thought he was present.

'My precious little nightingale,' said the gentleman-in-waiting, 'I have the honour to command your attendance at a court festival to-night, where you will charm his gracious majesty the emperor with your fascinating singing.'

'It sounds best among the trees,' said the nightingale, but it went with them willingly when it heard that the emperor wished it.

The palace had been brightened up for the occasion. The walls and the floors, which were all of china, shone by the light of many thousand golden lamps. The most beautiful flowers, all of the tinkling kind, were arranged in the corridors; there was hurrying to and fro, and a great draught, but this was just what made the bells ring; one's ears were full of the tinkling. In the middle of the large reception-room where the emperor sat a golden rod had been fixed, on which the nightingale was to perch. The whole court was assembled, and the little kitchen-maid had been permitted to stand behind the door, as she now had the actual title of cook. They were all dressed in their best; everybody's eyes were turned towards the little grey bird at which the emperor was nodding. The nightingale sang delightfully, and the tears came into the emperor's eyes, nay, they rolled down his cheeks; and then the nightingale sang more beautifully than ever, its notes touched all hearts. The emperor was charmed, and said the

'Is it possible?' said the gentleman-in-waiting. 'I should never have thought it was like that. How common it looks. Seeing so many grand people must have frightened all its colours away.'

M

nightingale should have his gold slipper to wear round its neck. But the nightingale declined with thanks; it had already been sufficiently rewarded.

'I have seen tears in the eyes of the emperor; that is my richest reward. The tears of an emperor have a wonderful power! God knows I am sufficiently recompensed!' and then it again burst into its sweet heavenly song.

'That is the most delightful coquetting I have ever seen!' said the ladies, and they took some water into their mouths to try and make the same gurgling when any one spoke to them, thinking so to equal the nightingale. Even the lackeys and the chambermaids announced that they were satisfied, and that is saying a great deal; they are always the most difficult people to please. Yes, indeed, the nightingale had made a sensation. It was to stay at court now, and to have its own cage, as well as liberty to walk out twice a day, and once in the night. It always had twelve footmen, with each one holding a ribbon which was tied round its leg. There was not much pleasure in an outing of that sort.

The whole town talked about the marvellous bird, and if two people met, one said to the other 'Night,' and the other answered 'Gale,' and then they sighed, perfectly understanding each other. Eleven cheesemongers' children were called after it, but they had not got a voice among them.

One day a large parcel came for the emperor; outside was written the word 'Nightingale.'

'Here we have another new book about this celebrated bird,' said the emperor. But it was no book; it was a little work of art in a box, an artificial nightingale, exactly like the living one, but it was studded all over with diamonds, rubies and sapphires.

When the bird was wound up it could sing one of the songs the real one sang, and it wagged its tail, which glittered with silver and gold. A ribbon was tied round its neck on which was written, 'The Emperor of Japan's nightingale is very poor compared to the Emperor of China's.'

Everybody said, 'Oh, how beautiful!' And the person who brought the artificial bird immediately received the title of Imperial Nightingale-Carrier in Chief.

'Now, they must sing together; what a duet that will be.'

Then they had to sing together, but they did not get on very well, for the real nightingale sang in its own way, and the artificial one could only sing waltzes.

'There is no fault in that,' said the music-master; 'it is perfectly in time and correct in every way!'

Then the artificial bird had to sing alone. It was just as great a success as the real one, and then it was so much prettier to look at; it glittered like bracelets and breast-pins.

It sang the same tune three and thirty times over, and yet it

[illegible]

Then it again burst into its sweet heavenly song.

'That is the most delightful coquetting I have ever seen!' said the ladies, and they took some water into their mouths to try and make the same gurgling, thinking so to equal the nightingale.

[illegible]

was not tired; people would willingly have heard it from the beginning again, but the emperor said that the real one must have a turn now—but where was it? No one had noticed that it had flown out of the open window, back to its own green woods.

'But what is the meaning of this?' said the emperor.

All the courtiers railed at it, and said it was a most ungrateful bird.

'We have got the best bird though,' said they, and then the artificial bird had to sing again, and this was the thirty-fourth time that they heard the same tune, but they did not know it thoroughly even yet, because it was so difficult.

The music-master praised the bird tremendously, and insisted that it was much better than the real nightingale, not only as regarded the outside with all the diamonds, but the inside too.

'Because you see, my ladies and gentlemen, and the emperor before all, in the real nightingale you never know what you will hear, but in the artificial one everything is decided beforehand! So it is, and so it must remain, it can't be otherwise. You can account for things, you can open it and show the human ingenuity in arranging the waltzes, how they go, and how one note follows upon another!'

'Those are exactly my opinions,' they all said, and the music-master got leave to show the bird to the public next Sunday. They were also to hear it sing, said the emperor. So they heard it, and all became as enthusiastic over it as if they had drunk themselves merry on tea, because that is a thoroughly Chinese habit.

Then they all said 'Oh,' and stuck their forefingers in the air and nodded their heads; but the poor fishermen who had heard the real nightingale said, 'It sounds very nice, and it is very like the real one, but there is something wanting, we don't know what.' The real nightingale was banished from the kingdom.

The artificial bird had its place on a silken cushion, close to the emperor's bed: all the presents it had received of gold and precious jewels were scattered round it. Its title had risen to be 'Chief Imperial Singer of the Bed-Chamber,' in rank number one, on the left side; for the emperor reckoned that side the important one, where the heart was seated. And even an emperor's heart is on the left side. The music-master wrote five-and-twenty volumes about the artificial bird; the treatise was very long and written in all the most difficult Chinese characters. Everybody said they had read and understood it, for otherwise they would have been reckoned stupid, and then their bodies would have been trampled upon.

Things went on in this way for a whole year. The emperor, the court, and all the other Chinamen knew every little gurgle in the song of the artificial bird by heart; but they liked it all the better for this, and they could all join in the song themselves.

[illegible]

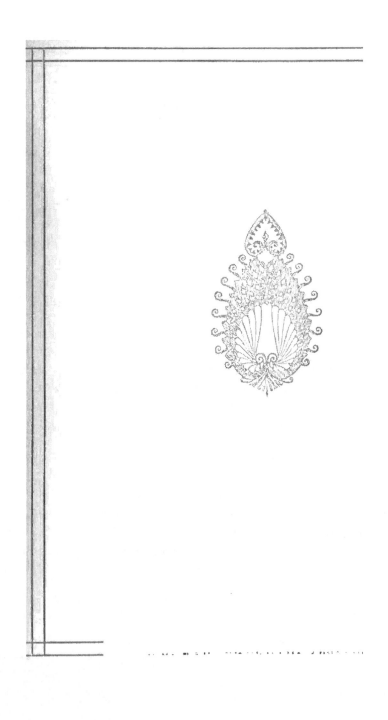

The music-master wrote five-and-twenty volumes about the artificial bird; the treatise was very long and written in all the most difficult Chinese characters.

[illegible]

Even the street boys sang 'zizizi' and 'cluck, cluck, cluck,' and the emperor sang it too.

But one evening when the bird was singing its best, and the emperor was lying in bed listening to it, something gave way inside the bird with a 'whizz.' Then a spring burst, 'whirr' went all the wheels, and the music stopped. The emperor jumped out of bed and sent for his private physicians, but what good could they do? Then they sent for the watchmaker, and after a good deal of talk and examination he got the works to go again somehow; but he said it would have to be saved as much as possible, because it was so worn out, and he could not renew the works so as to be sure of the tune. This was a great blow! They only dared to let the artificial bird sing once a year, and hardly that; but then the music-master made a little speech, using all the most difficult words. He said it was just as good as ever, and his saying it made it so.

Five years now passed, and then a great grief came upon the nation, for they were all very fond of their emperor, and he was ill and could not live, it was said. A new emperor was already chosen, and people stood about in the street, and asked the gentleman-in-waiting how their emperor was going on.

'P,' answered he, shaking his head.

The emperor lay pale and cold in his gorgeous bed, the courtiers thought he was dead, and they all went off to pay their respects to their new emperor. The lackeys ran off to talk matters over, and the chambermaids gave a great coffee-party. Cloth had been laid down in all the rooms and corridors so as to deaden the sound of footsteps, so it was very, very quiet. But the emperor was not dead yet. He lay stiff and pale in the gorgeous bed with its velvet hangings and heavy golden tassels. There was an open window high above him, and the moon streamed in upon the emperor, and the artificial bird beside him.

The poor emperor could hardly breathe, he seemed to have a weight on his chest, he opened his eyes, and then he saw that it was Death sitting upon his chest, wearing his golden crown. In one hand he held the emperor's golden sword, and in the other his imperial banner. Round about, from among the folds of the velvet hangings peered many curious faces: some were hideous, others gentle and pleasant. They were all the emperor's good and bad deeds, which now looked him in the face when Death was weighing him down.

'Do you remember that?' whispered one after the other; 'Do you remember this?' and they told him so many things that the perspiration poured down his face.

'I never knew that,' said the emperor. 'Music, music, sound the great Chinese drums!' he cried, 'that I may not hear what they are saying.' But they went on and on, and Death sat nodding his head, just like a Chinaman, at everything that was said.

'Music, music!' shrieked the emperor. 'You precious little

golden bird, sing, sing! I have loaded you with precious stones, and even hung my own golden slipper round your neck; sing, I tell you, sing!'

But the bird stood silent; there was nobody to wind it up, so of course it could not go. Death continued to fix the great empty sockets of his eyes upon him, and all was silent, so terribly silent.

Suddenly, close to the window, there was a burst of lovely song; it was the living nightingale, perched on a branch outside. It had heard of the emperor's need, and had come to bring comfort and hope to him. As it sang the faces round became fainter and fainter, and the blood coursed with fresh vigour in the emperor's veins and through his feeble limbs. Even Death himself listened to the song and said, 'Go on, little nightingale, go on!'

'Yes, if you give me the gorgeous golden sword; yes, if you give me the imperial banner; yes, if you give me the emperor's crown.'

And Death gave back each of these treasures for a song, and the nightingale went on singing. It sang about the quiet churchyard, when the roses bloom, where the elder flower scents the air, and where the fresh grass is ever moistened anew by the tears of the mourner. This song brought to Death a longing for his own garden, and, like a cold grey mist, he passed out of the window.

'Thanks, thanks!' said the emperor; 'you heavenly little bird, I know you! I banished you from my kingdom, and yet you have charmed the evil visions away from my bed by your song, and even Death away from my heart! How can I ever repay you?'

'You have rewarded me,' said the nightingale. 'I brought the tears to your eyes, the very first time I ever sang to you, and I shall never forget it! Those are the jewels which gladden the heart of a singer;—but sleep now, and wake up fresh and strong! I will sing to you!'

Then it sang again, and the emperor fell into a sweet refreshing sleep. The sun shone in at his window, when he woke refreshed and well; none of his attendants had yet come back to him, for they thought he was dead, but the nightingale still sat there singing.

'You must always stay with me!' said the emperor. 'You shall only sing when you like, and I will break the artificial bird into a thousand pieces!'

'Don't do that!' said the nightingale, 'it did all the good it could! keep it as you have always done! I can't build my nest and live in this palace, but let me come whenever I like, then I will sit on the branch in the evening, and sing to you. I will sing to cheer you and to make you thoughtful too; I will sing to you of the happy ones, and of those that suffer too. I will sing about the good and the evil, which are kept hidden from you. The little singing bird flies far and wide, to the poor fisherman, and the peasant's home, to numbers who are far from you and your court. I love your heart more than your crown, and yet there is an odour

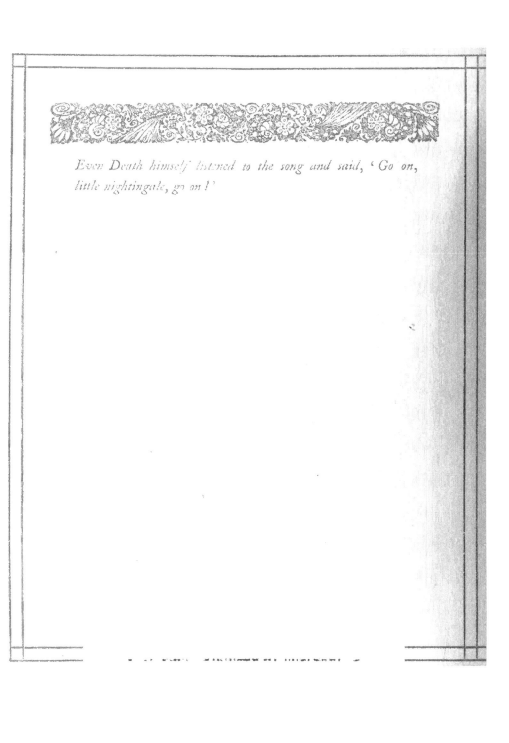

Even Death himself listened to the song and said, 'Go on, little nightingale, go on!'

[illegible]

of sanctity round the crown too!—I will come, and I will sing to you!—But you must promise me one thing!'—

'Everything!' said the emperor, who stood there in his imperial robes which he had just put on, and he held the sword heavy with gold upon his heart.

'One thing I ask you! Tell no one that you have a little bird who tells you everything; it will be better so!'

Then the nightingale flew away. The attendants came in to see after their dead emperor, and there he stood, bidding them 'Good morning!'

THE REAL PRINCESS

THERE was once a prince, and he wanted a princess, but then she must be a *real* Princess. He travelled right round the world to find one, but there was always something wrong. There were plenty of princesses, but whether they were real princesses he had great difficulty in discovering; there was always something which was not quite right about them. So at last he had to come home again, and he was very sad because he wanted a real princess so badly.

One evening there was a terrible storm; it thundered and lightened and the rain poured down in torrents; indeed it was a fearful night.

In the middle of the storm somebody knocked at the town gate, and the old King himself went to open it.

It was a princess who stood outside, but she was in a terrible state from the rain and the storm. The water streamed out of her hair and her clothes; it ran in at the top of her shoes and out at the heel, but she said that she was a real princess.

'Well we shall soon see if that is true,' thought the old Queen, but she said nothing. She went into the bedroom, took all the bedclothes off and laid a pea on the bedstead: then she took twenty mattresses and piled them on the top of the pea, and then twenty feather beds on the top of the mattresses. This was where the princess was to sleep that night. In the morning they asked her how she had slept.

'Oh terribly badly!' said the princess. 'I have hardly closed my eyes the whole night! Heaven knows what was in the bed. I seemed to be lying upon some hard thing, and my whole body is black and blue this morning. It is terrible!'

They saw at once that she must be a real princess when she had felt the pea through twenty mattresses and twenty feather beds. Nobody but a real princess could have such a delicate skin.

So the prince took her to be his wife, for now he was sure that he had found a real princess, and the pea was put into the Museum, where it may still be seen if no one has stolen it.

Now this is a true story.

THE GARDEN OF PARADISE

THERE was once a king's son; nobody had so many or such beautiful books as he had. He could read about everything which had ever happened in this world, and see it all represented in the most beautiful pictures. He could get information about every nation and every country; but as to where the Garden of Paradise was to be found, not a word could he discover, and this was the very thing he thought most about. His grandmother had told him, when he was quite a little fellow and was about to begin his school life, that every flower in the Garden of Paradise was a delicious cake, and that the pistils were full of wine. In one flower history was written, in another geography or tables; you had only to eat the cake and you knew the lesson. The more you ate, the more history, geography and tables you knew. All this he believed then; but as he grew older and wiser and learnt more, he easily perceived that the delights of the Garden of Paradise must be far beyond all this.

His grandmother had told him, when he was quite a little fellow and was about to begin his school life, that every flower in the Garden of Paradise was a delicious cake, and that the pistils were full of wine.

'Oh, why did Eve take of the tree of knowledge? Why did Adam eat the forbidden fruit? If it had only been I it would not have happened! never would sin have entered the world!'

This is what he said then, and he still said it when he was seventeen; his thoughts were full of the Garden of Paradise.

He walked into the wood one day; he was alone, for that was his greatest pleasure. Evening came on, the clouds drew up and it rained as if the whole heaven had become a sluice from which the water poured in sheets; it was as dark as it is otherwise in the deepest well. Now he slipped on the wet grass, and then he fell on the bare stones which jutted out of the rocky ground. Everything was dripping, and at last the poor Prince hadn't got a dry thread on him. He had to climb over huge rocks where the water oozed out of the thick moss. He was almost fainting; just then he heard a curious murmuring and saw in front of him a big lighted cave. A fire was burning in the middle, big enough to roast a stag, which was in fact being done; a splendid stag with its huge antlers was stuck on a spit, being slowly turned round between the hewn trunks of two fir trees. An oldish woman, tall and strong enough to be a man dressed up, sat by the fire throwing on logs from time to time.

'Come in, by all means!' she said; 'sit down by the fire so that your clothes may dry!'

'There is a shocking draught here,' said the Prince, as he sat down on the ground.

'It will be worse than this when my sons come home!' said the woman. 'You are in the cavern of the winds; my sons are the four winds of the world! Do you understand?'

'Who are your sons?' asked the Prince.

'Well that's not so easy to answer when the question is stupidly put,' said the woman. 'My sons do as they like; they are playing rounders now with the clouds up there in the great hall,' and she pointed up into the sky.

'Oh indeed!' said the Prince. 'You seem to speak very harshly, and you are not so gentle as the women I generally see about me!'

'Oh, I daresay they have nothing else to do! I have to be harsh if I am to keep my boys under control! But I can do it, although they are a stiff-necked lot! Do you see those four sacks hanging on the wall? They are just as frightened of them as you used to be of the cane behind the looking-glass. I can double the boys up, I can tell you, and then they have to go into the bag; we don't stand upon ceremony, and there they have to stay; they can't get out to play their tricks till it suits me to let them. But here we have one of them.' It was the Northwind who came in with an icy blast; great hailstones peppered about the floor and snow-flakes drifted in. He was dressed in bearskin trousers and jacket, and he had a sealskin cap drawn over his ears. Long icicles were hanging from his beard, and one hailstone after another dropped down from the collar of his jacket.

'Don't go straight to the fire,' said the Prince. 'You might easily get chilblains!'

'Chilblains!' said the Northwind with a loud laugh. 'Chilblains! they are my greatest delight! What sort of a feeble creature are you? How did you get into the cave of the winds?'

'He is my guest,' said the old woman, 'and if you are not pleased with that explanation you may go into the bag! Now you know my opinion!'

This had its effect, and the Northwind told them where he came from, and where he had been for the last month.

'I come from the Arctic seas,' he said. 'I have been on Behring Island with the Russian walrus-hunters. I sat at the helm and slept when they sailed from the north cape, and when I woke now and then the stormy petrels were flying about my legs. They are queer birds; they give a brisk flap with their wings and then keep them stretched out and motionless, and even then they have speed enough.'

'Pray don't be too long-winded,' said the mother of the winds. 'So at last you got to Behring Island!'

'It's perfectly splendid! There you have a floor to dance upon, as flat as a pancake, half-thawed snow, with moss. There were bones of whales and Polar bears lying about; they looked like the legs and arms of giants covered with green mould. One would think that the sun had never shone on them. I gave a little puff to the fog so that one could see the shed. It was a house built of wreckage and covered with the skins of whales; the flesh side was turned outwards; it was all red and green; a living Polar bear sat on the roof growling. I went to the shore and looked at the birds' nests, looked at the unfledged young ones screaming and gaping; then I blew down thousands of their throats and they learnt to shut their mouths. Lower down the walruses were rolling about like monster maggots with pigs' heads and teeth a yard long!'

'You're a good story-teller, my boy!' said his mother. 'It makes my mouth water to hear you!'

'Then there was a hunt! The harpoons were plunged into the walruses' breasts, and the steaming blood spurted out of them like fountains over the ice. Then I remembered my part of the game! I blew up and made my ships, the mountain-high icebergs, nip the boats; whew! how they whistled and how they screamed, but I whistled louder. They were obliged to throw the dead walruses, chests and ropes out upon the ice! I shook the snow-flakes over them and let them drift southwards to taste the salt water. They will never come back to Behring Island!'

'Then you've been doing evil!' said the mother of the winds.

'What good I did, the others may tell you,' said he. 'But here we have my brother from the west; I like him best of all; he smells of the sea and brings a splendid cool breeze with him!'

'Is that the little Zephyr?' asked the Prince.

'Yes, certainly it is Zephyr, but he is not so little as all that. He used to be a pretty boy once, but that's gone by!'

He looked like a wild man of the woods, but he had a padded hat on so as not to come to any harm. He carried a mahogany club cut in the American mahogany forests. It could not be anything less than that.

'Where do you come from?' asked his mother.

'From the forest wildernesses!' he said, 'where the thorny creepers make a fence between every tree, where the water-snake lies in the wet grass, and where human beings seem to be superfluous!'

'What did you do there?'

'I looked at the mighty river, saw where it dashed over the rocks in dust and flew with the clouds to carry the rainbow. I saw the wild buffalo swimming in the river, but the stream carried him away; he floated with the wild duck, which soared into the sky at the rapids; but the buffalo was carried over with the water. I liked that and blew a storm, so that the primæval trees had to sail too, and they were whirled about like shavings.'

'And you have done nothing else?' asked the old woman.

'I have been turning somersaults in the Savannahs, patting the wild horse, and shaking down cocoanuts! Oh yes, I have plenty of stories to tell! But one need not tell everything. You know that very well, old woman!' and then he kissed his mother so heartily that she nearly fell backwards; he was indeed a wild boy.

The Southwind appeared now in a turban and a flowing bedouin's cloak.

'It is fearfully cold in here,' he said, throwing wood on the fire; 'it is easy to see that the Northwind got here first!'

'It is hot enough here to roast a polar bear,' said the Northwind.

'You are a polar bear yourself!' said the Southwind.

'Do you want to go into the bag?' asked the old woman. 'Sit down on that stone and tell us where you have been.'

'In Africa, mother!' he answered. 'I have been chasing the lion with the Hottentots in Kaffirland! What grass there is on those plains! as green as an olive. The gnu was dancing about, and the ostriches ran races with me, but I am still the fastest. I went to the desert with its yellow sand. It looks like the bottom of the sea. I met a caravan! They were killing their last camel to get water to drink, but it wasn't much they got. The sun was blazing above, and the sand burning below. There were no limits to the outstretched desert. Then I burrowed into the fine loose sand and whirled it up in great columns—that was a dance! You should have seen how despondently the dromedaries stood, and the merchant drew his caftan over his head. He threw himself down before me as if I had been Allah, his god. Now they are buried, and there is a pyramid of sand over them all; when I blow it away, sometime the sun will bleach their bones, and then travellers will see that people have been there before, otherwise you would hardly believe it in the desert!'

'Then you have only been doing harm!' said the mother. 'Into the bag you go!' And before he knew where he was she had the Southwind by the waist and in the bag; it rolled about on the ground, but she sat down upon it and then it had to be quiet.

'Your sons are lively fellows!' said the Prince.

'Yes, indeed,' she said; 'but I can master them! Here comes the fourth.'

It was the Eastwind, and he was dressed like a Chinaman.

'Oh, have you come from that quarter?' said the mother. 'I thought you had been in the Garden of Paradise.'

'I am only going there to-morrow!' said the Eastwind. 'It will be a hundred years to-morrow since I have been there. I have just come from China, where I danced round the porcelain tower till all the bells jingled. The officials were flogged in the streets, the bamboo canes were broken over their shoulders, and they were all people ranging from the first to the ninth rank. They shrieked

"Many thanks, Father and benefactor," but they didn't mean what they said, and I went on ringing the bells and singing "Tsing, tsang, tsu!"'

'You're quite uproarious about it!' said the old woman. 'It's a good thing you are going to the Garden of Paradise to-morrow; it always has a good effect on your behaviour. Mind you drink deep of the well of wisdom, and bring a little bottleful home to me.'

'That I will,' said the Eastwind. 'But why have you put my brother from the south into the bag? Out with him. He must tell me about the phœnix; the Princess always wants to hear about that bird when I call every hundred years. Open the bag! then you'll be my sweetest mother, and I'll give you two pockets full of tea as green and fresh as when I picked it!'

'Well, for the sake of the tea, and because you are my darling, I will open my bag!'

She did open it and the Southwind crept out, but he was quite crestfallen because the strange Prince had seen his disgrace.

'Here is a palm leaf for the Princess!' said the Southwind. 'The old phœnix, the only one in the world, gave it to me. He has scratched his whole history on it with his bill, for the hundred years of his life, and she can read it for herself. I saw how the phœnix set fire to his nest himself and sat on it while it burnt, like the widow of a Hindoo. Oh, how the dry branches crackled, how it smoked, and what a smell there was! At last it all burst into flame; the old bird was burnt to ashes, but his egg lay glowing in the fire; it broke with a loud bang and the young one flew out. Now it rules over all the birds, and it is the only phœnix in the world. He bit a hole in the leaf I gave you; that is his greeting to the Princess.'

'Let us have something to eat now!' said the mother of the winds; and they all sat down to eat the roast stag, and the Prince sat by the side of the Eastwind, so they soon became good friends.

'I say,' said the Prince, 'just tell me who is this Princess, and where is the Garden of Paradise?'

'Oh ho!' said the Eastwind, 'if that is where you want to go you must fly with me to-morrow. But I may as well tell you that no human being has been there since Adam and Eve's time. You know all about them I suppose from your Bible stories?'

'Of course,' said the Prince.

'When they were driven away the Garden of Eden sank into the ground, but it kept its warm sunshine, its mild air, and all its charms. The queen of the fairies lives there. The Island of Bliss, where death never enters, and where living is a delight, is there. Get on my back to-morrow and I will take you with me; I think I can manage it! But you mustn't talk now, I want to go to sleep.'

When the Prince woke up in the early morning, he was not a little surprised to find that he was already high above the clouds.

He was sitting on the back of the Eastwind, who was holding him carefully; they were so high up that woods and fields, rivers and lakes, looked like a large coloured map.

'Good morning,' said the Eastwind. 'You may as well sleep a little longer, for there is not much to be seen in this flat country below us, unless you want to count the churches. They look like chalk dots on the green board.'

He called the fields and meadows 'the green board.'

'It was very rude of me to leave without saying good-bye to your mother and brothers,' said the Prince.

'One is excused when one is asleep!' said the Eastwind, and they flew on faster than ever. You could mark their flight by the rustling of the trees as they passed over the woods; and whenever they crossed a lake, or the sea, the waves rose and the great ships dipped low down in the water, like floating swans. Towards evening the large towns were amusing as it grew dark, with all their lights twinkling now here, now there, just as when one burns a piece of paper and sees all the little sparks like children coming home from school. The Prince clapped his hands, but the Eastwind told him he had better leave off and hold tight, or he might fall and find himself hanging on to a church steeple.

The eagle in the great forest flew swiftly, but the Eastwind flew more swiftly still. The Kossack on his little horse sped fast over the plains, but the Prince sped faster still.

The eagle in the great forest flew swiftly, but the Eastwind flew more swiftly still.

[illegible]

Now you can see the Himalayas!' said the Eastwind. 'They are the highest mountains in Asia; we shall soon reach the Garden of Paradise.'

They took a more southerly direction, and the air became scented with spices and flowers. Figs and pomegranates grew wild, and the wild vines were covered with blue and green grapes. They both descended here and stretched themselves on the soft grass, where the flowers nodded to the wind, as much as to say, 'Welcome back.'

'Are we in the Garden of Paradise now?' asked the Prince.

'No, certainly not!' answered the Eastwind. 'But we shall soon be there. Do you see that wall of rock and the great cavern where the wild vine hangs like a big curtain? We have to go through there! Wrap yourself up in your cloak, the sun is burning here, but a step further on it is icy cold. The bird which flies past the cavern has one wing out here in the heat of summer, and the other is there in the cold of winter.'

'So that is the way to the Garden of Paradise!' said the Prince.

Now they entered the cavern. Oh, how icily cold it was; but it did not last long. The Eastwind spread his wings, and they shone like the brightest flame; but what a cave it was! Large blocks of stone, from which the water dripped, hung over them in the most extraordinary shapes; at one moment it was so low and narrow that they had to crawl on hands and knees, the next it was as wide and lofty as if they were in the open air. It looked like a chapel of the dead, with mute organ pipes and petrified banners.

'We seem to be journeying along Death's road to the Garden of Paradise!' said the Prince, but the Eastwind never answered a word, he only pointed before them where a beautiful blue light was shining. The blocks of stone above them grew dimmer and dimmer, and at last they became as transparent as a white cloud in the moonshine. The air was also deliciously soft, as fresh as on the mountain-tops and as scented as down among the roses in the valley.

A river ran there as clear as the air itself, and the fish in it were like gold and silver. Purple eels, which gave out blue sparks with every curve, gambolled about in the water; and the broad leaves of the water-lilies were tinged with the hues of the rainbow, while the flower itself was like a fiery orange flame, nourished by the water, just as oil keeps a lamp constantly burning. A firm bridge of marble, as delicately and skilfully carved as if it were lace and glass beads, led over the water to the Island of Bliss, where the Garden of Paradise bloomed.

The Eastwind took the Prince in his arms and bore him over. The flowers and leaves there sang all the beautiful old songs of his childhood, but sang them more wonderfully than any human voice could sing them.

Were these palm trees or giant water plants growing here? The Prince had never seen such rich and mighty trees. The most wonderful climbing plants hung in wreaths, such as are only to be found pictured in gold and colours on the margins of old books of the Saints or entwined among their initial letters. It was the most extraordinary combination of birds, flowers and scrolls.

Close by on the grass stood a flock of peacocks with their brilliant tails outspread. Yes, indeed, it seemed so, but when the Prince touched them he saw that they were not birds but plants. They were big dock leaves, which shone like peacocks' tails. Lions and tigers sprang like agile cats among the green hedges, which were scented with the blossom of the olive, and the lion and the tiger were tame. The wild dove, glistening like a pearl, beat the lion's mane with his wings; and the antelope, otherwise so shy, stood by nodding, just as if he wanted to join the game.

The Fairy of the Garden now advanced to meet them; her garments shone like the sun, and her face beamed like that of a happy mother rejoicing over her child. She was young and very beautiful, and was surrounded by a band of lovely girls, each with a gleaming star in her hair.

When the Eastwind gave her the inscribed leaf from the Phœnix her eyes sparkled with delight. She took the Prince's hand and led him into her palace, where the walls were the colour of the brightest tulips in the sunlight. The ceiling was one great shining flower, and the longer one gazed into it the deeper the calyx seemed to be. The Prince went to the window, and looking through one of the panes saw the Tree of Knowledge, with the Serpent, and Adam and Eve standing by.

'Are they not driven out?' he asked, and the Fairy smiled, and explained that Time had burned a picture into each pane, but not of the kind one usually sees; they were alive, the leaves on the trees moved, and people came and went like the reflections in a mirror.

Then he looked through another pane, and he saw Jacob's dream, with the ladder going straight up into heaven, and angels with great wings were fluttering up and down. All that had ever happened in this world lived and moved on these window panes; only Time could imprint such wonderful pictures.

The Fairy smiled and led him into a large, lofty room, the walls of which were like transparent paintings of faces, one more beautiful than the other. These were millions of the Blessed who smiled and sang, and all their songs melted into one perfect melody. The highest ones were so tiny that they seemed smaller than the very smallest rosebud, no bigger than a pinpoint in a drawing. In the middle of the room stood a large tree, with handsome drooping branches; golden apples, large and small, hung like oranges among its green leaves. It was the Tree of

[illegible]

The Fairy of the Garden now advanced to meet them; her garments shone like the sun, and her face beamed like that of a happy mother rejoicing over her child.

[illegible]

Knowledge, of whose fruit Adam and Eve had eaten. From every leaf hung a shining red drop of dew; it was as if the tree wept tears of blood.

'Now let us get into the boat,' said the Fairy. 'We shall find refreshment on the swelling waters. The boat rocks, but it does not move from the spot; all the countries of the world will pass before our eyes.'

It was a curious sight to see the whole coast move. Here came lofty snow-clad Alps, with their clouds and dark fir trees. The horn echoed sadly among them, and the shepherd yodelled sweetly in the valleys. Then banian trees bent their long drooping branches over the boat, black swans floated on the water, and the strangest animals and flowers appeared on the shore. This was New Holland, the fifth portion of the world, which glided past them with a view of its blue mountains. They heard the song of priests, and saw the dances of the savages to the sound of drums and pipes of bone. The pyramids of Egypt reaching to the clouds, with fallen columns, and Sphynxes half buried in sand, next sailed past them. Then came the Aurora Borealis blazing over the peaks of the north; they were fireworks which could not be imitated. The Prince was so happy, and he saw a hundred times more than we have described.

'Can I stay here always?' he asked.

'That depends upon yourself,' answered the Fairy. 'If you

do not, like Adam, allow yourself to be tempted to do what is forbidden, you can stay here always.'

'I will not touch the apples on the Tree of Knowledge,' said the Prince. 'There are thousands of other fruits here as beautiful.'

'Test yourself, and if you are not strong enough, go back with the Eastwind who brought you. He is going away now, and will not come back for a hundred years; the time will fly in this place like a hundred hours, but that is a long time for temptation and sin. Every evening when I leave you I must say, "Come with me," and I must beckon to you, but stay behind. Do not come with me, for with every step you take your longing will grow stronger. You will reach the hall where grows the Tree of Knowledge; I sleep beneath its fragrant drooping branches. You will bend over me and I must smile, but if you press a kiss upon my lips Paradise will sink deep down into the earth, and it will be lost to you. The sharp winds of the wilderness will whistle round you, the cold rain will drop from your hair. Sorrow and labour will be your lot.'

'I will remain here!' said the Prince.

And the Eastwind kissed him on the mouth and said: 'Be strong, then we shall meet again in a hundred years. Farewell! Farewell!' And the Eastwind spread his great wings; they shone like poppies at the harvest time, or the Northern Lights in a cold winter.

'Good-bye! good-bye!' whispered the flowers. Storks and pelicans flew in a line like waving ribbons, conducting him to the boundaries of the Garden.

'Now we begin our dancing!' said the Fairy; 'at the end when I dance with you, as the sun goes down you will see me beckon to you and cry, "Come with me"; but do not come. I have to repeat it every night for a hundred years. Every time you resist, you will grow stronger, and at last you will not even think of following. To-night is the first time. Remember my warning!'

And the Fairy led him into a large hall of white transparent lilies, the yellow stamens in each formed a little golden harp which echoed the sound of strings and flutes. Lovely girls, slender and lissom, dressed in floating gauze, which revealed their exquisite limbs, glided in the dance, and sang of the joy of living—that they would never die—and that the Garden of Paradise would bloom for ever.

The sun went down and the sky was bathed in golden light which gave the lilies the effect of roses; and the Prince drank of the foaming wine handed to him by the maidens. He felt such joy as he had never known before; he saw the background of the hall opening where the Tree of Knowledge stood in a radiancy which blinded him. The song proceeding from it was soft and lovely, like his mother's voice, and she seemed to say, 'My child, my beloved child!'

Then the Fairy beckoned to him and said so tenderly, 'Come with me,' that he rushed towards her, forgetting his promise, forgetting everything on the very first evening that she smiled and beckoned to him.

The fragrance in the scented air around grew stronger, the harps sounded sweeter than ever, and it seemed as if the millions of smiling heads in the hall where the Tree grew nodded and sang, 'One must know everything. Man is lord of the earth.' They were no longer tears of blood which fell from the Tree; it seemed to him that they were red shining stars.

'Come with me, come with me,' spoke those trembling tones, and at every step the Prince's cheeks burnt hotter and hotter and his blood coursed more rapidly.

'I must go,' he said, 'it is no sin; I must see her asleep; nothing will be lost if I do not kiss her, and that I will not do. My will is strong.'

The Fairy dropped her shimmering garment, drew back the branches, and a moment after was hidden within their depths.

'I have not sinned yet!' said the Prince, 'nor will I'; then he drew back the branches. There she lay asleep already, beautiful as only the Fairy in the Garden of Paradise can be. She smiled in her dreams; he bent over her and saw the tears welling up under her eyelashes.

'Do you weep for me?' he whispered. 'Weep not, beautiful

T [illegible]

The Fairy dropped her shimmering garment, drew back the branches, and a moment after was hidden within their depths.

[illegible]

maiden. I only now understand the full bliss of Paradise; it surges through my blood and through my thoughts. I feel the strength of the angels and of everlasting life in my mortal limbs! If it were to be everlasting night to me, a moment like this were worth it!' and he kissed away the tears from her eyes; his mouth touched hers.

Then came a sound like thunder, louder and more awful than any he had ever heard before, and everything around collapsed. The beautiful Fairy, the flowery Paradise sank deeper and deeper. The Prince saw it sink into the darkness of night; it shone far off like a little tiny twinkling star. The chill of death crept over his limbs; he closed his eyes and lay long as if dead.

The cold rain fell on his face, and the sharp wind blew around his head, and at last his memory came back. 'What have I done?' he sighed. 'I have sinned like Adam, sinned so heavily that Paradise has sunk low beneath the earth!' And he opened his eyes; he could still see the star, the far-away star, which twinkled like Paradise; it was the morning star in the sky. He got up and found himself in the wood near the cave of the winds, and the mother of the winds sat by his side. She looked angry and raised her hand.

'So soon as the first evening!' she said. 'I thought as much; if you were my boy, you should go into the bag!'

'Ah, he shall soon go there!' said Death. He was a strong

old man, with a scythe in his hand and great black wings. 'He shall be laid in a coffin, but not now; I only mark him and then leave him for a time to wander about on the earth to expiate his sin and to grow better. I will come some time. When he least expects me, I shall come back, lay him in a black coffin, put it on my head, and fly to the skies. The Garden of Paradise blooms there too, and if he is good and holy he shall enter into it; but if his thoughts are wicked and his heart still full of sin, he will sink deeper in his coffin than Paradise sank, and I shall only go once in every thousand years to see if he is to sink deeper or to rise to the stars, the twinkling stars up there.'

THE MERMAID

FAR out at sea the water is as blue as the bluest cornflower, and as clear as the clearest crystal; but it is very deep, too deep for any cable to fathom, and if many steeples were piled on the top of one another they would not reach from the bed of the sea to the surface of the water. It is down there that the Mermen live.

Now don't imagine that there are only bare white sands at the bottom; oh no! the most wonderful trees and plants grow there, with such flexible stalks and leaves, that at the slightest motion of the water they move just as if they were alive. All the fish, big and little, glide among the branches just as, up here, birds glide through the air. The palace of the Merman King lies in the very deepest part; its walls are of coral and the long pointed windows of the clearest amber, but the roof is made of mussel shells which open and shut with the lapping of the water. This has a lovely effect, for there are gleaming pearls in every shell, any one of which would be the pride of a queen's crown.

THE MERMAID

The Merman King had been for many years a widower, but his old mother kept house for him; she was a clever woman, but so proud of her noble birth that she wore twelve oysters on her tail, while the other grandees were only allowed six. Otherwise she was worthy of all praise, especially because she was so fond of the little mermaid princesses, her grandchildren. They were six beautiful children, but the youngest was the prettiest of all; her skin was as soft and delicate as a roseleaf, her eyes as blue as the deepest sea, but like all the others she had no feet, and instead of legs she had a fish's tail.

All the livelong day they used to play in the palace in the great halls, where living flowers grew out of the walls. When the great amber windows were thrown open the fish swam in, just as the swallows fly into our rooms when we open the windows, but the fish swam right up to the little princesses, ate out of their hands, and allowed themselves to be patted.

Outside the palace was a large garden, with fiery red and deep blue trees, the fruit of which shone like gold, while the flowers glowed like fire on their ceaselessly waving stalks. The ground was of the finest sand, but it was of a blue phosphorescent tint. Everything was bathed in a wondrous blue light down there; you might more readily have supposed yourself to be high up in the air, with only the sky above and below you, than that you were at the bottom of the ocean. In a dead calm you could just catch a

v

[illegible]

The Merman King had been for many years a widower, but his old mother kept house for him; she was a clever woman, but so proud of her noble birth that she wore twelve oysters on her tail, while the other grandees were only allowed six.

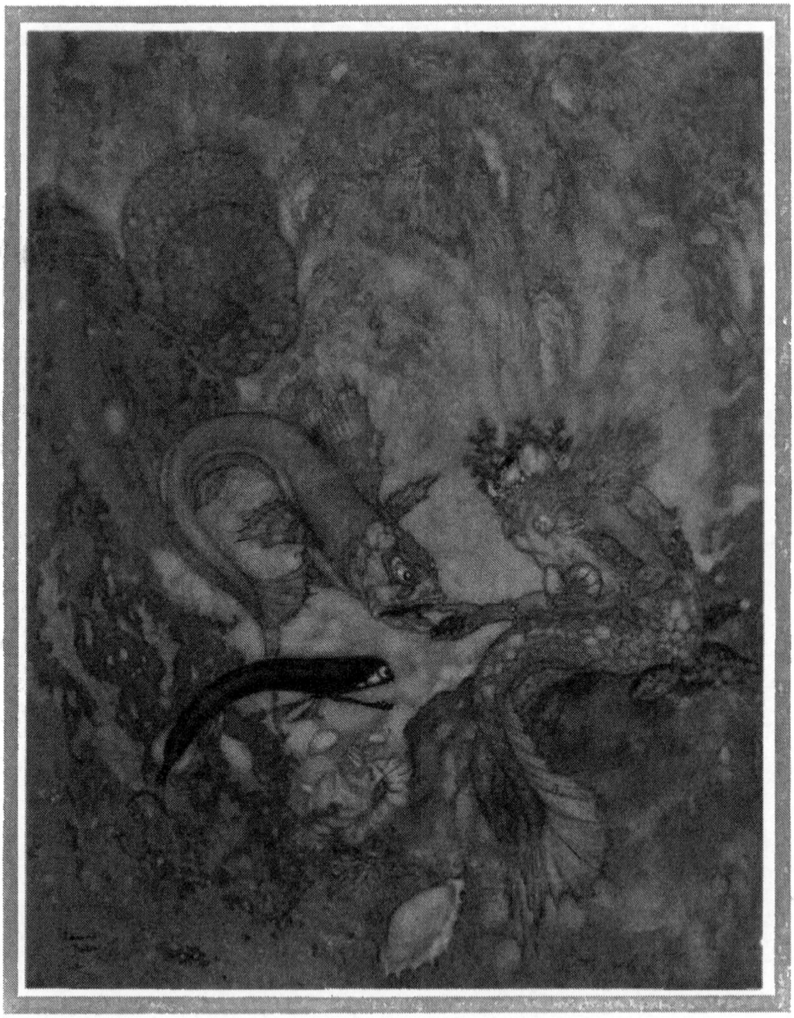

[illegible]

glimpse of the sun like a purple flower with a stream of light radiating from its calyx.

Each little princess had her own little plot of garden, where she could dig and plant just as she liked. One made her flower-bed in the shape of a whale; another thought it nice to have hers like a little mermaid; but the youngest made hers quite round like the sun, and she would only have flowers of a rosy hue like its beams. She was a curious child, quiet and thoughtful, and while the other sisters decked out their gardens with all kinds of extraordinary objects which they got from wrecks, she would have nothing besides the rosy flowers like the sun up above, except a statue of a beautiful boy. It was hewn out of the purest white marble and had gone to the bottom from some wreck. By the statue she planted a rosy red weeping willow which grew splendidly, and the fresh delicate branches hung round and over it, till they almost touched the blue sand where the shadows showed violet, and were ever moving like the branches. It looked as if the leaves and the roots were playfully interchanging kisses.

Nothing gave her greater pleasure than to hear about the world of human beings up above; she made her old grandmother tell her all that she knew about ships and towns, people and animals. But above all it seemed strangely beautiful to her that up on the earth the flowers were scented, for they were not so at the bottom of the sea; also that the woods were green, and that the fish which were to be seen among the branches could sing so loudly and sweetly that it was a delight to listen to them. You see the grandmother called little birds fish, or the mermaids would not have understood her, as they had never seen a bird.

'When you are fifteen,' said the grandmother, 'you will be allowed to rise up from the sea and sit on the rocks in the moonlight, and look at the big ships sailing by, and you will also see woods and towns.'

One of the sisters would be fifteen in the following year, but the others,—well, they were each one year younger than the other, so that the youngest had five whole years to wait before she would be allowed to come up from the bottom, to see what things were like on earth. But each one promised the others to give a full account of all that she had seen, and found most wonderful on the first day. Their grandmother could never tell them enough, for there were so many things about which they wanted information.

None of them was so full of longings as the youngest, the very one who had the longest time to wait, and who was so quiet and dreamy. Many a night she stood by the open windows and looked up through the dark blue water which the fish were lashing with their tails and fins. She could see the moon and the stars, it is true; their light was pale, but they looked much bigger through the water than they do to our eyes. When she saw a dark shadow glide between her and them, she knew that it was either a whale swimming above her, or else a ship laden with human beings. I am certain they never dreamt that a lovely little mermaid was standing down below, stretching up her white hands towards the keel.

The eldest princess had now reached her fifteenth birthday, and was to venture above the water. When she came back she had hundreds of things to tell them, but the most delightful of all, she said, was to lie in the moonlight, on a sandbank in a calm sea, and to gaze at the large town close to the shore, where the lights twinkled like hundreds of stars; to listen to music and the noise and bustle of carriages and people, to see the many church towers and spires, and to hear the bells ringing; and just because she could not go on shore she longed for that most of all.

Oh, how eagerly the youngest sister listened! and when, later in the evening she stood at the open window and looked up through the dark blue water, she thought of the big town with all its noise and bustle, and fancied that she could even hear the church bells ringing.

The year after, the second sister was allowed to mount up through the water and swim about wherever she liked. The sun was just going down when she reached the surface, the most beautiful sight, she thought, that she had ever seen. The whole sky had looked like gold, she said, and as for the clouds! well, their beauty was beyond description; they floated in red and violet splendour over her head, and, far faster than they went, a flock of wild swans flew like a long white veil over the water towards the setting sun; she swam towards it, but it sank and all the rosy light on clouds and water faded away.

The year after that the third sister went up, and, being much the most venturesome of them all, swam up a broad river which ran into the sea. She saw beautiful green, vine-clad hills; palaces and country seats peeping through splendid woods. She heard the birds singing, and the sun was so hot that she was often obliged to dive, to cool her burning face. In a tiny bay she found a troop of little children running about naked and paddling in the water; she wanted to play with them, but they were frightened and ran away. Then a little black animal came up; it was a dog, but she had never seen one before; it barked so furiously at her that she was frightened and made for the open sea. She could never forget the beautiful woods, the green hills and the lovely children who could swim in the water although they had no fishes' tails.

The fourth sister was not so brave; she stayed in the remotest part of the ocean, and, according to her account, that was the most beautiful spot. You could see for miles and miles around you, and the sky above was like a great glass dome. She had seen ships, but only far away, so that they looked like sea-gulls. There were grotesque dolphins turning somersaults, and gigantic whales squirting water through their nostrils like hundreds of fountains on every side.

Now the fifth sister's turn came. Her birthday fell in the winter, so that she saw sights that the others had not seen on their first trips. The sea looked quite green, and large icebergs were floating about, each one of which looked like a pearl, she said, but was much bigger than the church towers built by men. They took the most wonderful shapes, aad sparkled like diamonds. She had seated herself on one of the largest, and all the passing ships sheered off in alarm when they saw her sitting there with her long hair streaming loose in the wind.

In the evening the sky became overcast with dark clouds; it thundered and lightened, and the huge icebergs glittering in the bright lightning, were lifted high into the air by the black waves. All the ships shortened sail, and there was fear and trembling on every side, but she sat quietly on her floating iceberg watching the blue lightning flash in zigzags down on to the shining sea.

The first time any of the sisters rose above the water she was delighted by the novelties and beauties she saw; but once grown up, and at liberty to go where she liked, she became indifferent and longed for her home; in the course of a month or so they all said that after all their own home in the deep was best, it was so cosy there.

Many an evening the five sisters interlacing their arms would rise above the water together. They had lovely voices, much clearer than any mortal, and when a storm was rising, and they expected ships to be wrecked, they would sing in the most seductive strains of the wonders of the deep, bidding the seafarers have no fear of them. But the sailors could not understand the words, they thought it was the voice of the storm; nor could it be theirs to see this Elysium of the deep, for when the ship sank they were drowned, and only reached the Merman's palace in death. When the elder sisters rose up in this manner, arm-in-arm, in the evening, the youngest remained behind quite alone, looking after them as if she must weep; but mermaids have no tears, and so they suffer all the more.

'Oh! if I were only fifteen!' she said, 'I know how fond I shall be of the world above, and of the mortals who dwell there.'

At last her fifteenth birthday came.

'Now we shall have you off our hands,' said her grandmother, the old queen-dowager. 'Come now, let me adorn you like your other sisters!' and she put a wreath of white lilies round her hair, but every petal of the flowers was half a pearl; then the old queen had eight oysters fixed on to the princess's tail to show her high rank.

'But it hurts so!' said the little mermaid.

'You must endure the pain for the sake of the finery!' said her grandmother.

But oh! how gladly would she have shaken off all this splendour, and laid aside the heavy wreath. Her red flowers in her garden suited her much better, but she did not dare to make any alteration. 'Good-bye,' she said, and mounted as lightly and airily as a bubble through the water.

The sun had just set when her head rose above the water, but the clouds were still lighted up with a rosy and golden splendour, and the evening star sparkled in the soft pink sky, the air was mild and fresh, and the sea as calm as a millpond. A big three-masted ship lay close by with only a single sail set, for there was not a breath of wind, and the sailors were sitting about the rigging, on the cross-trees, and at the mast-heads. There was music and singing on board, and as the evening closed in hundreds of gaily coloured lanterns were lighted—they looked like the flags of all nations waving in the air. The little mermaid swam right up to the cabin windows, and every time she was lifted by the swell she could see through the transparent panes crowds of gaily dressed people. The handsomest of them all was the young prince with large dark eyes; he could not be much more than sixteen, and all these festivities were in honour of his birthday. The sailors danced on deck, and when the prince appeared among them hundreds of rockets were let off making it as light as day, and frightening the little mermaid so much that she had to dive under the water. She soon ventured up again, and it was just as if all the stars of heaven were falling in showers round about her. She had never seen such magic fires. Great suns whirled round, gorgeous fire-fish hung in the blue air, and all was reflected in the calm and glassy sea. It was so light on board the ship that every little rope could be seen, and the people still better. Oh, how handsome the prince was! how he laughed and smiled as he greeted his guests, while the music rang out in the quiet night.

It got quite late, but the little mermaid could not take her eyes off the ship and the beautiful prince. The coloured lanterns were put out, no more rockets were sent up, and the cannon had ceased its thunder, but deep down in the sea there was a dull murmuring and moaning sound. Meanwhile she was rocked up and down on the waves, so that she could look into the cabin; but the ship got more and more way on, sail after sail was filled by the wind, the waves grew stronger, great clouds gathered, and it lightened in the distance. Oh, there was going to be a fearful storm! and soon the sailors had to shorten sail. The great ship rocked and rolled as she dashed over the angry sea, the black waves rose like mountains, high enough to overwhelm her, but she dived like a swan through them and rose again and again on their towering crests. The little mermaid thought it a most amusing race, but not so the sailors. The ship creaked and groaned; the mighty timbers bulged and bent under the heavy blows; the water broke over the decks, snapping the main mast like a reed; she heeled over on her side, and the water rushed into the hold.

Now the little mermaid saw that they were in danger, and she had for her own sake to beware of the floating beams and wreckage. One moment it was so pitch dark that she could not see at all, but when the lightning flashed it became so light that she could see all on board. Every man was looking out for his own safety as best he could; but she more particularly followed the young prince with her eyes, and when the ship went down she saw him sink in the deep sea. At first she was quite delighted, for now he was coming to be with her, but then she remembered that human beings could not live under water, and that only if he were dead could he go to her father's palace. No! he must not die; so she swam towards him all among the drifting beams and planks, quite forgetting that they might crush her. She dived deep down under the water, and came up again through the waves, and at last reached the young prince just as he was becoming unable to swim any further in the stormy sea. His limbs were numbed, his beautiful eyes were closing, and he must have died if the little mermaid had not come to the rescue. She held his head above the water and let the waves drive them whithersoever they would.

By daybreak all the storm was over, of the ship not a trace was to be seen; the sun rose from the water in radiant brilliance, and his rosy beams seemed to cast a glow of life into the prince's cheeks, but his eyes remained closed. The mermaid kissed his fair and lofty brow, and stroked back the dripping hair; it seemed to her that he was like the marble statue in her little garden; she kissed him again and longed that he might live.

At last she saw dry land before her, high blue mountains on whose summits the white snow glistened as if a flock of swans had settled there; down by the shore were beautiful green woods, and in the foreground a church or temple, she did not quite know which, but it was a building of some sort. Lemon and orange trees grew in the garden, and lofty palms stood by the gate. At this point the sea formed a little bay where the water was quite calm, but very deep, right up to the cliffs; at their foot was a strip of fine white sand to which she swam with the beautiful prince, and laid him down on it, taking great care that his head should rest high up in the warm sunshine.

The bells now began to ring in the great white building, and a number of young maidens came into the garden. Then the little mermaid swam further off behind some high rocks and covered her hair and breast with foam, so that no one should see her little face, and then she watched to see who would discover the poor prince.

It was not long before one of the maidens came up to him. At first she seemed quite frightened, but only for a moment, and then she fetched several others, and the mermaid saw that the prince was coming to life, and that he smiled at all those around him, but he never smiled at her. You see he did not know that she

His limbs were numbed, his beautiful eyes were closing, and he must have died if the little mermaid had not come to the rescue.

had saved him. She felt so sad that when he was led away into the great building she dived sorrowfully into the water and made her way home to her father's palace.

Always silent and thoughtful, she became more so now than ever. Her sisters often asked her what she had seen on her first visit to the surface, but she never would tell them anything.

Many an evening and many a morning she would rise to the place where she had left the prince. She saw the fruit in the garden ripen, and then gathered, she saw the snow melt on the mountain-tops, but she never saw the prince, so she always went home still sadder than before. At home her only consolation was to sit in her little garden with her arms twined round the handsome marble statue which reminded her of the prince. It was all in gloomy shade now, as she had ceased to tend her flowers, and the garden had become a neglected wilderness of long stalks and leaves entangled with the branches of the tree.

At last she could not bear it any longer, so she told one of her sisters, and from her it soon spread to the others, but to no one else except to one or two other mermaids who only told their dearest friends. One of these knew all about the prince; she had also seen the festivities on the ship; she knew where he came from and where his kingdom was situated.

'Come, little sister!' said the other princesses, and, throwing their arms round each other's shoulders, they rose from the water in a long line, just in front of the prince's palace.

It was built of light yellow glistening stone, with great marble staircases, one of which led into the garden. Magnificent gilded cupolas rose above the roof, and the spaces between the columns which encircled the building were filled with life-like marble statues. Through the clear glass of the lofty windows you could see gorgeous halls adorned with costly silken hangings, and the pictures on the walls were a sight worth seeing. In the midst of the central hall a large fountain played, throwing its jets of spray upwards to a glass dome in the roof, through which the sunbeams lighted up the water and the beautiful plants which grew in the great basin.

She knew now where he lived, and often used to go there in the evenings and by night over the water. She swam much nearer the land than any of the others dared; she even ventured right up the narrow channel under the splendid marble terrace which threw a long shadow over the water. She used to sit here looking at the young prince, who thought he was quite alone in the clear moonlight.

She saw him many an evening sailing about in his beautiful boat, with flags waving and music playing; she used to peep through the green rushes, and if the wind happened to catch her long silvery veil and any one saw it, they only thought it was a swan flapping its wings.

Many a night she heard the fishermen, who were fishing by torchlight, talking over the good deeds of the young prince; and she was happy to think that she had saved his life when he was drifting about on the waves, half dead, and she could not forget how closely his head had pressed her breast, and how passionately she had kissed him; but he knew nothing of all this, and never saw her even in his dreams.

She became fonder and fonder of mankind, and longed more and more to be able to live among them; their world seemed so infinitely bigger than hers; with their ships they could scour the ocean, they could ascend the mountains high above the clouds, and their wooded, grass-grown lands extended further than her eye could reach. There was so much that she wanted to know, but her sisters could not give an answer to all her questions, so she asked her old grandmother, who knew the upper world well, and rightly called it the country above the sea.

'If men are not drowned,' asked the little mermaid, 'do they live for ever? Do they not die as we do down here in the sea?'

'Yes,' said the old lady, 'they have to die too, and their lifetime is even shorter than ours. We may live here for three hundred years, but when we cease to exist we become mere foam on the water and do not have so much as a grave among our dear ones. We have no immortal souls; we have no future life; we are just like the green sea-weed, which, once cut down, can never revive again! Men, on the other hand, have a soul which lives for ever, lives after the body has become dust; it rises through the clear air, up to the shining stars! Just as we rise from the water to see the land of mortals, so they rise up to unknown beautiful regions which we shall never see.'

'Why have we no immortal souls?' asked the little mermaid sadly. 'I would give all my three hundred years to be a human being for one day, and afterwards to have a share in the heavenly kingdom.'

'You must not be thinking about that,' said the grandmother; 'we are much better off and happier than human beings.'

'Then I shall have to die and to float as foam on the water, and never hear the music of the waves or see the beautiful flowers or the red sun! Is there nothing I can do to gain an immortal soul?'

'No,' said the grandmother; 'only if a human being so loved you that you were more to him than father or mother, if all his thoughts and all his love were so centred in you that he would let the priest join your hands and would vow to be faithful to you here, and to all eternity; then your body would become infused with his soul. Thus, and only thus, could you gain a share in the felicity of mankind. He would give you a soul while yet keeping his own. But that can never happen! That which is your greatest beauty in the sea, your fish's tail, is thought hideous up on earth, so little do they understand about it; to be pretty there you must have two clumsy supports which they call legs!'

Then the little mermaid sighed and looked sadly at her fish's tail.

'Let us be happy,' said the grandmother; 'we will hop and skip during our three hundred years of life; it is surely a long enough time; and after it is over we shall rest all the better in our graves. There is to be a court ball to-night.'

This was a much more splendid affair than we ever see on earth. The walls and the ceiling of the great ballroom were of thick but transparent glass. Several hundreds of colossal mussel shells, rose red and grass green, were ranged in order round the sides holding blue lights, which illuminated the whole room and shone through the walls, so that the sea outside was quite lit up. You could see countless fish, great and small, swimming towards the glass walls, some with shining scales of crimson hue, while others were golden and silvery. In the middle of the room was a broad stream of running water, and on this the mermaids and mermen danced to their own beautiful singing. No earthly beings have such lovely voices. The little mermaid sang more sweetly than any of them, and they all applauded her. For a moment she felt glad at heart, for she knew that she had the finest voice either in the sea or on land. But she soon began to think again about the upper world, she could not forget the handsome prince and her sorrow in not possessing, like him, an immortal soul. Therefore she stole out of her father's palace, and while all within was joy and merriment, she sat sadly in her little garden. Suddenly she heard the sound of a horn through the water, and she thought, 'Now he is out sailing up there; he whom I love more than father or mother, he to whom my thoughts cling and to whose hands I am ready to commit the happiness of my life. I will dare anything to win him and to gain an immortal soul! While my sisters are dancing in my father's palace I will go to the sea-witch, of whom I have always been very much afraid; she will perhaps be able to advise and help me!'

Thereupon the little mermaid left the garden and went towards the roaring whirlpools at the back of which the witch lived. She had never been that way before; no flowers grew there, no seaweed, only the bare grey sands, stretched towards the whirlpools, which like rushing mill-wheels swirled round, dragging everything that came within reach down to the depths. She had to pass between these boiling eddies to reach the witch's domain, and for a long way the only path led over warm bubbling mud, which the witch called her 'peat bog.' Her house stood behind this in the midst of a weird forest. All the trees and bushes were polyps, half animal and half plant; they looked like hundred-headed snakes growing out of the sand, the branches were long slimy arms, with tentacles like wriggling worms, every joint of which, from the root to the outermost tip, was in constant motion. They wound themselves tightly round whatever they could lay hold of and never let it escape. The little mermaid standing outside was quite frightened, her heart beat fast with terror and she nearly turned back, but then she remembered the prince and the immortal soul of mankind and took courage. She bound her long flowing hair tightly round her head, so that the polyps should not seize her by it, folded her hands over her breast, and darted like a fish through the water, in between the hideous polyps, which stretched out their sensitive arms and tentacles towards her. She could see that every one of them had something or other, which they had grasped with their hundred arms, and which they held as if in iron bands. The bleached bones of men who had perished at sea and sunk below peeped forth from the arms of some, while others clutched rudders and sea-chests, or the skeleton of some land animal; and most horrible of all, a little mermaid whom they had caught and suffocated. Then she came to a large opening in the wood where the ground was all slimy, and where some huge fat water snakes were gambolling about. In the middle of this opening was a house built of the bones of the wrecked; there sat the witch, letting a toad eat out of her mouth, just as mortals let a little canary eat sugar. She called the hideous water snakes her little chickens, and allowed them to crawl about on her unsightly bosom.

'I know very well what you have come here for,' said the witch. 'It is very foolish of you! all the same you shall have your way, because it will lead you into misfortune, my fine princess. You want to get rid of your fish's tail, and instead to have two stumps to walk about upon like human beings, so that the young prince may fall in love with you, and that you may win him and an immortal soul.' Saying this, she gave such a loud hideous laugh that the toad and the snakes fell to the ground and wriggled about there.

'You are just in the nick of time,' said the witch; 'after sunrise to-morrow I should not be able to help you until another year had run its course. I will make you a potion, and before sunrise you must swim ashore with it, seat yourself on the beach and drink it; then your tail will divide and shrivel up to what men call beautiful legs. But it hurts; it is as if a sharp sword were running through you. All who see you will say that you are the most beautiful child of man they have ever seen. You will keep your gliding gait, no dancer will rival you, but every step you take will be as if you were treading upon sharp knives, so sharp as to draw blood. If you are willing to suffer all this I am ready to help you!'

'Yes!' said the little princess with a trembling voice, thinking of the prince and of winning an undying soul.

'But remember,' said the witch, 'when once you have received a human form, you can never be a mermaid again; you will never again be able to dive down through the water to your sisters and to your father's palace. And if you do not succeed in winning the prince's love, so that for your sake he will forget father and mother, cleave to you with his whole heart, let the priest join your hands and make you man and wife, you will gain no immortal soul! The first morning after his marriage with another your heart will break, and you will turn into foam of the sea.'

'I will do it,' said the little mermaid as pale as death.

'But you will have to pay me, too,' said the witch, 'and it is no trifle that I demand. You have the most beautiful voice of any at the bottom of the sea, and I daresay that you think you will fascinate him with it; but you must give me that voice; I will have the best you possess in return for my precious potion! I have to mingle my own blood with it so as to make it as sharp as a two-edged sword.'

'But if you take my voice,' said the little mermaid, 'what have I left?'

'Your beautiful form,' said the witch, 'your gliding gait, and your speaking eyes; with these you ought surely to be able to bewitch a human heart. Well! have you lost courage? Put out your little tongue, and I will cut it off in payment for the powerful draught.'

'Let it be done,' said the little mermaid, and the witch put on her caldron to brew the magic potion. 'There is nothing like cleanliness,' said she, as she scoured the pot with a bundle of snakes; then she punctured her breast and let the black blood drop into the caldron, and the steam took the most weird shapes, enough to frighten any one. Every moment the witch threw new ingredients into the pot, and when it boiled the bubbling was like the sound of crocodiles weeping. At last the potion was ready and it looked like the clearest water.

'There it is,' said the witch, and thereupon she cut off the tongue of the little mermaid, who was dumb now and could neither sing nor speak.

'If the polyps should seize you, when you go back through my wood,' said the witch, 'just drop a single drop of this liquid on them, and their arms and fingers will burst into a thousand pieces.' But the little mermaid had no need to do this, for at the mere sight of the bright liquid, which sparkled in her hand like a shining star, they drew back in terror. So she soon got past the wood, the bog, and the eddying whirlpools.

She saw her father's palace; the lights were all out in the great ballroom, and no doubt all the household was asleep, but she did not dare to go in now that she was dumb and about to leave her home for ever. She felt as if her heart would break with grief. She stole into the garden and plucked a flower from each of her sisters' plots, wafted with her hand countless kisses towards the palace, and then rose up through the dark blue water.

But the little mermaid had no need to do this, for at the mere sight of the bright liquid which sparkled in her hand like a shining star, they drew back in terror.

The sun had not risen when she came in sight of the prince's palace and landed at the beautiful marble steps. The moon was shining bright and clear. The little mermaid drank the burning, stinging draught, and it was like a sharp, two-edged sword running through her tender frame; she fainted away and lay as if she were dead. When the sun rose on the sea she woke up and became conscious of a sharp pang, but just in front of her stood the handsome young prince, fixing his coal black eyes on her; she cast hers down and saw that her fish's tail was gone, and that she had the prettiest little white legs any maiden could desire; but she was quite naked, so she wrapped her long thick hair around her. The prince asked who she was and how she came there. She looked at him tenderly and with a sad expression in her dark blue eyes, but could not speak. Then he took her by the hand and led her into the palace. Every step she took was, as the witch had warned her beforehand, as if she were treading on sharp knives and spikes, but she bore it gladly; led by the prince, she moved as lightly as a bubble, and he and every one else marvelled at her graceful gliding gait.

Clothed in the costliest silks and muslins she was the greatest beauty in the palace, but she was dumb, and could neither sing nor speak. Beautiful slaves clad in silks and gold came forward and sang to the prince and his royal parents; one of them sang better than all the others, and the prince clapped his hands and smiled at her ; that made the little mermaid very sad, for she knew that she used to sing far better herself. She thought, 'Oh! if he only knew that for the sake of being with him I had given up my voice for ever!' Now the slaves began to dance, graceful undulating dances to enchanting music ; thereupon the little mermaid, lifting her beautiful white arms and raising herself on tiptoe, glided on the floor with a grace which none of the other dancers had yet attained. With every motion her grace and beauty became more apparent, and her eyes appealed more deeply to the heart than the songs of the slaves. Every one was delighted with it, especially the prince, who called her his little foundling ; and she danced on and on, notwithstanding that every time her foot touched the ground it was like treading on sharp knives. The prince said that she should always be near him, and she was allowed to sleep outside his door on a velvet cushion.

He had a man's dress made for her, so that she could ride about with him. They used to ride through scented woods, where the green branches brushed her shoulders, and little birds sang among the fresh leaves. She climbed up the highest mountains with the prince, and although her delicate feet bled so that others saw it, she only laughed and followed him until they saw the clouds sailing below them like a flock of birds, taking flight to distant lands.

At home in the prince's palace, when at night the others were

[illegible]

The prince asked who she was and how she came there; she looked at him tenderly and with a sad expression in her dark blue eyes, but could not speak.

[illegible]

asleep, she used to go out on to the marble steps; it cooled her burning feet to stand in the cold sea-water, and at such times she used to think of those she had left in the deep.

One night her sisters came arm in arm; they sang so sorrowfully as they swam on the water that she beckoned to them, and they recognised her, and told her how she had grieved them all. After that they visited her every night, and one night she saw, a long way out, her old grandmother (who for many years had not been above the water), and the Merman King with his crown on his head; they stretched out their hands towards her, but did not venture so close to land as her sisters.

Day by day she became dearer to the prince; he loved her as one loves a good sweet child, but it never entered his head to make her his queen; yet unless she became his wife she would never win an everlasting soul, but on his wedding morning would turn to sea-foam.

'Am I not dearer to you than any of them?' the little mermaid's eyes seemed to say when he took her in his arms and kissed her beautiful brow.

'Yes, you are the dearest one to me,' said the prince, 'for you have the best heart of them all, and you are fondest of me; you are also like a young girl I once saw, but whom I never expect to see again. I was on board a ship which was wrecked; I was driven on shore by the waves close to a holy Temple where several young girls were ministering at a service; the youngest of them found me on the beach and saved my life; I saw her but twice. She was the only person I could love in this world, but you are like her, you almost drive her image out of my heart. She belongs to the holy Temple, and therefore by good fortune you have been sent to me; we will never part!'

'Alas! he does not know that it was I who saved his life,' thought the little mermaid. 'I bore him over the sea to the wood where the Temple stands. I sat behind the foam and watched to see if any one would come. I saw the pretty girl he loves better than me.' And the mermaid heaved a bitter sigh, for she could not weep.

'The girl belongs to the holy Temple, he has said; she will never return to the world, they will never meet again. I am here with him; I see him every day. Yes! I will tend him, love him, and give up my life to him.'

But now the rumour ran that the prince was to be married to the beautiful daughter of a neighbouring king, and for that reason was fitting out a splendid ship. It was given out that the prince was going on a voyage to see the adjoining countries, but it was without doubt to see the king's daughter; he was to have a great suite with him. But the little mermaid shook her head and laughed; she knew the prince's intentions much better than any of the others. 'I must take this voyage,' he had said to her;

'I must go and see the beautiful princess; my parents demand that, but they will never force me to bring her home as my bride; I can never love her! She will not be like the lovely girl in the Temple whom you resemble. If ever I had to choose a bride it would sooner be you with your speaking eyes, my sweet, dumb foundling!' And he kissed her rosy mouth, played with her long hair, and laid his head upon her heart, which already dreamt of human joys and an immortal soul.

'You are not frightened of the sea, I suppose, my dumb child?' he said, as they stood on the proud ship which was to carry them to the country of the neighbouring king; and he told her about storms and calms, about curious fish in the deep, and the marvels seen by divers; and she smiled at his tales, for she knew all about the bottom of the sea much better than any one else.

At night, in the moonlight, when all were asleep, except the steersman who stood at the helm, she sat at the side of the ship trying to pierce the clear water with her eyes, and fancied she saw her father's palace, and above it her old grandmother with her silver crown on her head, looking up through the cross currents towards the keel of the ship. Then her sisters rose above the water; they gazed sadly at her, wringing their white hands. She beckoned to them, smiled, and was about to tell them that all was going well and happily with her, when the cabin-boy approached, and the sisters dived down, but he supposed that the white objects he had seen were nothing but flakes of foam.

The next morning the ship entered the harbour of the neighbouring king's magnificent city. The church bells rang and trumpets were sounded from every lofty tower, while the soldiers paraded with flags flying and glittering bayonets. There was a *fête* every day, there was a succession of balls, and receptions followed one after the other, but the princess was not yet present; she was being brought up a long way off, in a holy Temple they said, and was learning all the royal virtues. At last she came. The little mermaid stood eager to see her beauty, and she was obliged to confess that a lovelier creature she had never beheld. Her complexion was exquisitely pure and delicate, and her trustful eyes of the deepest blue shone through their dark lashes.

'It is you,' said the prince, 'you who saved me when I lay almost lifeless on the beach?' and he clasped his blushing bride to his heart. 'Oh! I am too happy!' he exclaimed to the little mermaid.

'A greater joy than I had dared to hope for has come to pass. You will rejoice at my joy, for you love me better than any one.' Then the little mermaid kissed his hand, and felt as if her heart were broken already.

His wedding morn would bring death to her and change her to foam.

All the church bells pealed and heralds rode through the town proclaiming the nuptials. Upon every altar throughout the land fragrant oil was burnt in costly silver lamps. Amidst the swinging of censers by the priests the bride and bridegroom joined hands and received the bishop's blessing. The little mermaid dressed in silk and gold stood holding the bride's train, but her ears were deaf to the festal strains, her eyes saw nothing of the sacred ceremony; she was thinking of her coming death and of all that she had lost in this world.

That same evening the bride and bridegroom embarked, amidst the roar of cannon and the waving of banners. A royal tent of purple and gold softly cushioned was raised amidships where the bridal pair were to repose during the calm cool night.

The sails swelled in the wind and the ship skimmed lightly and almost without motion over the transparent sea.

At dusk lanterns of many colours were lighted and the sailors danced merrily on deck. The little mermaid could not help thinking of the first time she came up from the sea and saw the same splendour and gaiety; and she now threw herself among the dancers, whirling, as a swallow skims through the air when pursued. The onlookers cheered her in amazement, never had she danced so divinely; her delicate feet pained her as if they were cut with knives, but she did not feel it, for the pain at her heart was much sharper. She knew that it was the last night that she would breathe the same air as he, and would look upon the mighty deep, and the blue starry heavens; an endless night without thought and without dreams awaited her, who neither had a soul, nor could win one. The joy and revelry on board lasted till long past midnight; she went on laughing and dancing with the thought of death all the time in her heart. The prince caressed his lovely bride and she played with his raven locks, and with their arms entwined they retired to the gorgeous tent. All became hushed and still on board the ship, only the steersman stood at the helm; the little mermaid laid her white arms on the gunwale and looked eastwards for the pink-tinted dawn; the first sunbeam, she knew, would be her death. Then she saw her sisters rise from the water; they were as pale as she was; their beautiful long hair no longer floated on the breeze, for it had been cut off.

'We have given it to the witch to obtain her help, so that you may not die to-night! She has given us a knife; here it is, look how sharp it is! Before the sun rises, you must plunge it into the prince's heart, and when his warm blood sprinkles your feet they will join together and grow into a tail, and you will once more be a mermaid; you will be able to come down into the water to us, and to live out your three hundred years before you are turned into dead, salt sea-foam. Make haste! you or he must die before sunrise! Our old grandmother is so full of grief that her white hair has fallen off as ours fell under the witch's scissors. Slay the

Once more she looked at the prince, with her eyes already dimmed by death, then dashed overboard and fell, her body dissolving into foam.

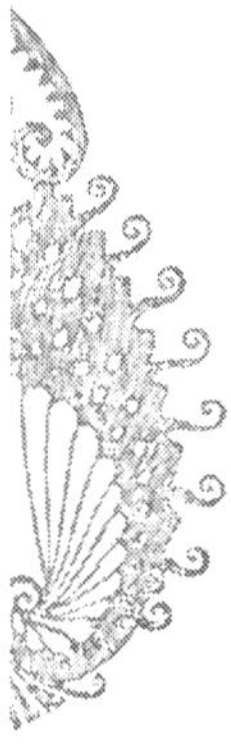

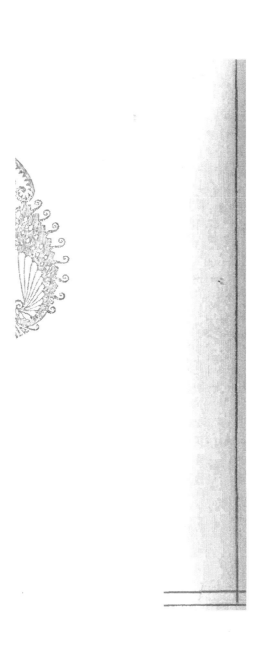

prince and come back to us! Quick! Quick! do you not see the rosy streak in the sky? In a few minutes the sun will rise and then you must die!' saying this they heaved a wondrous deep sigh and sank among the waves.

The little mermaid drew aside the purple curtain from the tent and looked at the beautiful bride asleep with her head on the prince's breast. She bent over him and kissed his fair brow, looked at the sky where the dawn was spreading fast, looked at the sharp knife, and again fixed her eyes on the prince, who, in his dream called his bride by name. Yes! she alone was in his thoughts! For a moment the knife quivered in her grasp, then she threw it far out among the waves, now rosy in the morning light, and where it fell the water bubbled up like drops of blood.

Once more she looked at the prince, with her eyes already dimmed by death, then dashed overboard and fell, her body dissolving into foam.

Now the sun rose from the sea and with its kindly beams warmed the deadly cold foam, so that the little mermaid did not feel the chill of death. She saw the bright sun, and above her floated hundreds of beauteous ethereal beings, through which she could see the white ship and the rosy heavens; their voices were melodious, but so spirit-like that no human ear could hear them, any more than earthly eye could see their forms. Light as bubbles they floated through the air without the aid of wings. The little mermaid perceived that she had a form like theirs; it gradually took shape out of the foam. 'To whom am I coming?' said she, and her voice sounded like that of the other beings, so unearthly in its beauty that no music of ours could reproduce it.

'To the daughters of the air!' answered the others; 'a mermaid has no undying soul, and can never gain one without winning the love of a human being. Her eternal life must depend upon an unknown power. Nor have the daughters of the air an everlasting soul, but by their own good deeds they may create one for themselves. We fly to the tropics where mankind is the victim of hot and pestilent winds; there we bring cooling breezes. We diffuse the scent of flowers all around, and bring refreshment and healing in our train. When, for three hundred years, we have laboured to do all the good in our power, we gain an undying soul and take a part in the everlasting joys of mankind. You, poor little mermaid, have with your whole heart struggled for the same thing as we have struggled for. You have suffered and endured, raised yourself to the spirit-world of the air, and now, by your own good deeds you may, in the course of three hundred years, work out for yourself an undying soul.'

Then the little mermaid lifted her transparent arms towards God's sun, and for the first time shed tears.

On board ship all was again life and bustle. She saw the prince with his lovely bride searching for her; they looked sadly at the bubbling foam, as if they knew that she had thrown herself into the waves. Unseen she kissed the bride on her brow, smiled at the prince, and rose aloft with the other spirits of the air to the rosy clouds which sailed above.

'In three hundred years we shall thus float into Paradise.'

'We might reach it sooner,' whispered one. 'Unseen we flit into those homes of men where there are children, and for every day that we find a good child who gives pleasure to its parents and deserves their love God shortens our time of probation. The child does not know when we fly through the room, and when we smile with pleasure at it one year of our three hundred is taken away. But if we see a naughty or badly disposed child, we cannot help shedding tears of sorrow, and every tear adds a day to the time of our probation.'

THE EMPEROR'S NEW CLOTHES

MANY years ago there was an Emperor, who was so excessively fond of new clothes that he spent all his money on them. He cared nothing about his soldiers, nor for the theatre, nor for driving in the woods except for the sake of showing off his new clothes. He had a costume for every hour in the day, and instead of saying, as one does about any other king or emperor, 'He is in his council chamber,' here one always said, 'The Emperor is in his dressing-room.'

Life was very gay in the great town where he lived; hosts of strangers came to visit it every day, and among them one day two swindlers. They gave themselves out as weavers, and said that they knew how to weave the most beautiful stuffs imaginable. Not only were the colours and patterns unusually fine, but the clothes that were made of the stuffs had the peculiar quality of becoming invisible to every person who was not fit for the office he held, or if he was impossibly dull.

'Those must be splendid clothes,' thought the Emperor. 'By wearing them I should be able to discover which men in my kingdom are unfitted for their posts. I shall distinguish the wise men from the fools. Yes, I certainly must order some of that stuff to be woven for me.

He paid the two swindlers a lot of money in advance so that they might begin their work at once.

They did put up two looms and pretended to weave, but they had nothing whatever upon their shuttles. At the outset they asked for a quantity of the finest silk and the purest gold thread, all of which they put into their own bags, while they worked away at the empty looms far into the night.

'I should like to know how those weavers are getting on with the stuff,' thought the Emperor; but he felt a little queer when he reflected that any one who was stupid or unfit for his post would not be able to see it. He certainly thought that he need have no fears for himself, but still he thought he would send somebody else first to see how it was getting on. Everybody in the town knew what wonderful power the stuff possessed, and every one was anxious to see how stupid his neighbour was.

'I will send my faithful old minister to the weavers,' thought the Emperor. 'He will be best able to see how the stuff looks, for he is a clever man, and no one fulfils his duties better than he does!'

So the good old minister went into the room where the two swindlers sat working at the empty loom.

'Heaven preserve us!' thought the old minister, opening his eyes very wide. 'Why, I can't see a thing!' But he took care not to say so.

Both the swindlers begged him to be good enough to step a little nearer, and asked if he did not think it a good pattern and beautiful colouring. They pointed to the empty loom, and the poor old minister stared as hard as he could, but he could not see anything, for of course there was nothing to see.

'Good heavens!' thought he, 'is it possible that I am a fool. I have never thought so, and nobody must know it. Am I not fit for my post? It will never do to say that I cannot see the stuffs.'

'Well, sir, you don't say anything about the stuff,' said the one who was pretending to weave.

'Oh, it is beautiful! quite charming!' said the old minister, looking through his spectacles; 'this pattern and these colours! I will certainly tell the Emperor that the stuff pleases me very much.'

'We are delighted to hear you say so,' said the swindlers, and then they named all the colours and described the peculiar pattern. The old minister paid great attention to what they said, so as to be able to repeat it when he got home to the Emperor.

Then the swindlers went on to demand more money, more

They pointed to the empty loom, and the poor old minister stared as hard as he could, but he could not see anything, for of course there was nothing to see.

silk, and more gold, to be able to proceed with the weaving; but they put it all into their own pockets—not a single strand was ever put into the loom, but they went on as before weaving at the empty loom.

The Emperor soon sent another faithful official to see how the stuff was getting on, and if it would soon be ready. The same thing happened to him as to the minister; he looked and looked, but as there was only the empty loom, he could see nothing at all.

'Is not this a beautiful piece of stuff?' said both the swindlers, showing and explaining the beautiful pattern and colours which were not there to be seen.

'I know I am not a fool!' thought the man, 'so it must be that I am unfit for my good post! It is very strange, though! However, one must not let it appear!' So he praised the stuff he did not see, and assured them of his delight in the beautiful colours and the originality of the design. 'It is absolutely charming!' he said to the Emperor. Everybody in the town was talking about this splendid stuff.

Now the Emperor thought he would like to see it while it was still on the loom. So, accompanied by a number of selected courtiers, among whom were the two faithful officials who had already seen the imaginary stuff, he went to visit the crafty impostors, who were working away as hard as ever they could at the empty loom.

'It is magnificent!' said both the honest officials. 'Only see, your Majesty, what a design! What colours!' And they pointed to the empty loom, for they thought no doubt the others could see the stuff.

'What!' thought the Emperor; 'I see nothing at all! This is terrible! Am I a fool? Am I not fit to be Emperor? Why, nothing worse could happen to me!'

'Oh, it is beautiful!' said the Emperor. 'It has my highest approval!' and he nodded his satisfaction as he gazed at the empty loom. Nothing would induce him to say that he could not see anything.

The whole suite gazed and gazed, but saw nothing more than all the others. However, they all exclaimed with his Majesty, 'It is very beautiful!' and they advised him to wear a suit made of this wonderful cloth on the occasion of a great procession which was just about to take place. 'It is magnificent! gorgeous! excellent! went from mouth to mouth; they were all equally delighted with it. The Emperor gave each of the rogues an order of knighthood to be worn in their buttonholes and the title of 'Gentlemen weavers.'

The swindlers sat up the whole night, before the day on which the procession was to take place, burning sixteen candles; so that people might see how anxious they were to get the Emperor's new clothes ready. They pretended to take the stuff off the loom. They cut it out in the air with a huge pair of scissors, and they

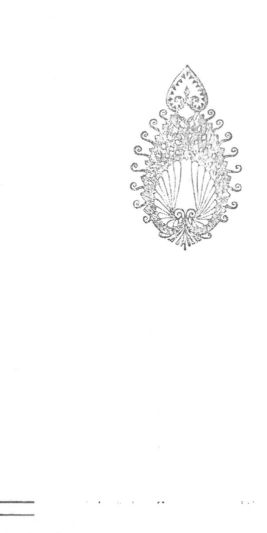

Then the emperor walked along in the procession under the gorgeous canopy, and everybody in the streets and at the windows exclaimed, 'How beautiful the Emperor's new clothes are!'

[illegible]

stitched away with needles without any thread in them. At last they said: 'Now the Emperor's new clothes are ready!'

The Emperor, with his grandest courtiers, went to them himself, and both the swindlers raised one arm in the air, as if they were holding something, and said: 'See, these are the trousers, this is the coat, here is the mantle!' and so on. 'It is as light as a spider's web. One might think one had nothing on, but that is the very beauty of it!'

'Yes!' said all the courtiers, but they could not see anything, for there was nothing to see.

'Will your imperial majesty be graciously pleased to take off your clothes,' said the impostors, 'so that we may put on the new ones, along here before the great mirror?'

The Emperor took off all his clothes, and the impostors pretended to give him one article of dress after the other of the new ones which they had pretended to make. They pretended to fasten something round his waist and to tie on something; this was the train, and the Emperor turned round and round in front of the mirror.

'How well his majesty looks in the new clothes! How becoming they are!' cried all the people round. 'What a design, and what colours! They are most gorgeous robes!'

'The canopy is waiting outside which is to be carried over your majesty in the procession,' said the master of the ceremonies.

'Well, I am quite ready,' said the Emperor. 'Don't the clothes fit well?' and then he turned round again in front of the mirror, so that he should seem to be looking at his grand things.

The chamberlains who were to carry the train stooped and pretended to lift it from the ground with both hands, and they walked along with their hands in the air. They dared not let it appear that they could not see anything.

Then the Emperor walked along in the procession under the gorgeous canopy, and everybody in the streets and at the windows exclaimed, 'How beautiful the Emperor's new clothes are! What a splendid train! And they fit to perfection!' Nobody would let it appear that he could see nothing, for then he would not be fit for his post, or else he was a fool.

None of the Emperor's clothes had been so successful before.

'But he has got nothing on,' said a little child.

'Oh, listen to the innocent,' said its father; and one person whispered to the other what the child had said. 'He has nothing on; a child says he has nothing on!'

'But he has nothing on!' at last cried all the people.

The Emperor writhed, for he knew it was true, but he thought 'the procession must go on now,' so held himself stiffer than ever, and the chamberlains held up the invisible train.

THE WIND'S TALE

ABOUT WALDEMAR DAA AND HIS DAUGHTERS

WHEN the wind sweeps across a field of grass it makes little ripples in it like a lake; in a field of corn it makes great waves like the sea itself: this is the wind's frolic. Then listen to the stories it tells; it sings them aloud, one kind of song among the trees of the forest, and a very different one when it is pent up within walls with all their cracks and crannies. Do you see how the wind chases the white fleecy clouds as if they were a flock of sheep? Do you hear the wind down there, howling in the open doorway like a watchman winding his horn? Then, too, how he whistles in the chimneys, making the fire crackle and sparkle. How cosy it is to sit in the warm glow of the fire listening to the tales it has to tell! Let the wind tell its own story! It can tell you more adventures than all of us put together. Listen now:—

'Whew!—Whew!—Fare away!' That was the refrain of his song.

THE WIND'S TALE

'Close to the Great Belt stands an old mansion with thick red walls,' says the wind. 'I know every stone of it; I knew them before when they formed part of Marsk Stig's Castle on the Ness. It had to come down. The stones were used again, and made a new wall of a new castle in another place—Borreby Hall as it now stands.

'I have watched the highborn men and women of all the various races who have lived there, and now I am going to tell you about Waldemar Daa and his daughters!

'He held his head very high, for he came of a royal stock! He knew more than the mere chasing of a stag, or the emptying of a flagon; he knew how to manage his affairs, he said himself.

'His lady wife walked proudly across the brightly polished floors, in her gold brocaded kirtle; the tapestries in the rooms were gorgeous, and the furniture of costly carved woods. She had brought much gold and silver plate into the house with her, and the cellars were full of German ale, when there was anything there at all. Fiery black horses neighed in the stables; Borreby Hall was a very rich place when wealth came there.

'Then there were the children, three dainty maidens, Ida, Johanna and Anna Dorothea. I remember their names well.

'They were rich and aristocratic people, and they were born and bred in wealth! Whew!—whew!—fare away!' roared the wind, then he went on with his story.

'I did not see here, as in other old noble castles the highborn lady sitting among her maidens in the great hall turning the spinning-wheel. No, she played upon the ringing lute, and sang to its tones. Her songs were not always the old Danish ditties, however, but songs in foreign tongues. All was life and hospitality; noble guests came from far and wide; there were sounds of music and the clanging of flagons, so loud that I could not drown them!' said the wind. 'Here were arrogance and ostentation enough and to spare; plenty of lords, but the Lord had no place there.

'Then came the evening of May-day!' said the wind. 'I came from the west; I had been watching ships being wrecked and broken up on the west coast of Jutland. I tore over the heaths and the green wooded coasts, across the island of Funen and over the Great Belt puffing and blowing. I settled down to rest on the coast of Zealand close to Borreby Hall, where the splendid forest of oaks still stood. The young bachelors of the neighbourhood came out and collected faggots and branches, the longest and driest they could find. These they took to the town, piled them up in a heap, and set fire to them; then the men and maidens danced and sang round the bonfire. I lay still,' said the wind, 'but I softly moved a branch, the one laid by the handsomest young man, and his billet blazed up highest of all. He was the chosen one, he had the name of honour, he became 'Buck of the Street!' and he chose from among the girls his little May-lamb. All was life and merriment, greater far than within rich Borreby Hall.

'The great lady came driving towards the Hall, in her gilded chariot drawn by six horses. She had her three dainty daughters with her; they were indeed three lovely flowers. A rose, a lily and a pale hyacinth. The mother herself was a gorgeous tulip; she took no notice whatever of the crowd, who all stopped in their game to drop their curtsies and make their bows; one might have thought that, like a tulip, she was rather frail in the stalk and feared to bend her back. The rose, the lily, and the pale hyacinth—yes, I saw them all three. Whose May-lambs were they one day to become, thought I; their mates would be proud knights—perhaps even princes!

'Whew!—whew!—fare away! Yes, the chariot bore them away, and the peasants whirled on in their dance. They played at "Riding the Summer into the village," to Borreby village, Tareby village, and many others.

'But that night when I rose,' said the wind, 'the noble lady laid herself down to rise no more; that came to her which comes to every one—there was nothing new about it. Waldemar Daa stood grave and silent for a time; "The proudest tree may bend, but it does not break," said something within him. The daughters wept, and every one else at the Castle was wiping their eyes; but Madam Daa had fared away, and I fared away too! Whew!—whew!' said the wind.

She played upon the ringing lute, and sang to its tones.

2 P

[illegible]

'I came back again; I often came back across the island of Funen and the waters of the Belt, and took up my place on Borreby shore close to the great forest of oaks. The ospreys and the wood pigeons used to build in it, the blue raven and even the black stork! It was early in the year; some of the nests were full of eggs, while in others the young ones were just hatched. What a flying and screaming was there! Then came the sound of the axe, blow upon blow; the forest was to be felled. Waldemar Daa was about to build a costly ship, a three-decked man-of-war, which it was expected the king would buy. So the wood fell, the ancient landmark of the seaman, the home of the birds. The shrike was frightened away; its nest was torn down; the osprey and all the other birds lost their nests too, and they flew about distractedly, shrieking in their terror and anger. The crows and the jackdaws screamed in mockery, Caw! caw! Waldemar Daa and his three daughters stood in the middle of the wood among the workmen. They all laughed at the wild cries of the birds, except Anna Dorothea, who was touched by their distress, and when they were about to fell a tree which was half-dead, and on whose naked branches a black stork had built its nest, out of which the young ones were sticking their heads, she begged them with tears in her eyes to spare it. So the tree with the black stork's nest was allowed to stand. It was only a little thing.

'The chopping and the sawing went on—the three-decker

was built. The master builder was a man of humble origin, but of noble loyalty; great power lay in his eyes and on his forehead, and Waldemar Daa liked to listen to him, and little Ida liked to listen too, the eldest fifteen-year-old daughter. But whilst he built the ship for her father, he built a castle in the air for himself, in which he and little Ida sat side by side as man and wife. This might also have happened if his castle had been built of solid stone, with moat and ramparts, wood and gardens. But with all his wisdom the shipbuilder was only a poor bird, and what business has a sparrow in a crane's nest? Whew! whew! I rushed away, and he rushed away, for he dared not stay, and little Ida got over it, as get over it she must.

'The fiery black horses stood neighing in the stables; they were worth looking at, and they were looked at to some purpose too. An admiral was sent from the King to look at the new man-of-war, with a view to purchasing it. The admiral was loud in his admiration of the horses. I heard all he said,' added the wind. 'I went through the open door with the gentlemen and scattered the straw like gold before their feet. Waldemar Daa wanted gold; the admiral wanted the black horses, and so he praised them as he did; but his hints were not taken, therefore the ship remained unsold. There it stood by the shore covered up with boards, like a Noah's Ark which never reached the water. Whew! whew! get along! get along! It was a miserable business. In the winter, when the fields were covered with snow and the Belt was full of ice-floes which I drove up on to the coast,' said the wind, 'the ravens and crows came in flocks, the one blacker than the other, and perched upon the desolate, dead ship by the shore. They screamed themselves hoarse about the forest which had disappeared, and the many precious birds' nests which had been devastated, leaving old and young homeless; and all for the sake of this old piece of lumber, the proud ship which was never to touch the water! I whirled the snow about till it lay in great heaps round the ship. I let it hear my voice, and all that a storm has to say. I know that I did my best to give it an idea of the sea. Whew! whew!'

'The winter passed by; winter and summer passed away! They come and go just as I do. The snow-flakes, the apple blossom, and the leaves fall, each in their turn. Whew! whew! they pass away, as men pass too!

'The daughters were still young. Little Ida, the rose, as lovely to look at as when the shipbuilder turned his gaze upon her. I often took hold of her long brown hair when she stood lost in thought by the apple-tree in the garden. She never noticed that I showered apple-blossom over her loosened hair; she only gazed at the red sunset against the golden background of the sky, and the dark trees and bushes of the garden. Her sister Johanna was like a tall, stately lily; she held herself as stiffly erect as her mother, and seemed to have the same dread of bending her stem. She liked to walk in the long gallery where the family portraits hung. The ladies were painted in velvet and silk, with tiny pearl embroidered caps on their braided tresses. Their husbands were all clad in steel, or in costly cloaks lined with squirrel skins and stiff blue ruffs; their swords hung loosely by their sides. Where would Johanna's portrait one day hang on these walls? What would her noble husband look like? These were her thoughts, and she even spoke them aloud; I heard her as I swept through the long corridor into the gallery, where I veered round again.

'Anna Dorothea, the pale hyacinth, was only a child of fourteen, quiet and thoughtful. Her large blue eyes, as clear as water, were very solemn, but childhood's smile still played upon her lips; I could not blow it away, nor did I wish to do so. I used to meet her in the garden, the ravine, and in the manor fields. She was always picking flowers and herbs, those she knew her father could use for healing drinks and potions. Waldemar Daa was proud and conceited, but he was also learned, and he knew a great deal about many things. One could see that, and many whispers went about as to his learning. The fire blazed in his stove even in summer, and his chamber door was locked. This went on for days and nights, but he did not talk much about it. One must deal silently with the forces of nature. He would soon discover the best of everything, the red, red gold!

'This was why his chimney flamed and smoked and sparkled. Yes, I was there, too,' said the wind.

I used to meet her in the garden, the ravine, and in the manor fields. She was always picking flowers and herbs, those she knew her father could use for healing drinks and potions.

[illegible]

'Away with you, away! I sang in the back of the chimney. Smoke, smoke, embers and ashes, that is all it will come to! You will burn yourself up in it. Whew! whew! away with it! But Waldemar Daa could not let it go.

'The fiery steeds in the stable, where were they? The old gold and silver plate in cupboard and chest, where was that? The cattle, the land, the castle itself? Yes, they could all be melted down in the crucible, but yet no gold would come.

'Barn and larder got emptier and emptier. Fewer servants; more mice. One pane of glass got broken and another followed it. There was no need for me to go in by the doors,' said the wind. 'A smoking chimney means a cooking meal, but the only chimney which smoked here swallowed up all the meals, all for the sake of the red gold.

'I blew through the castle gate like a watchman blowing his horn, but there was no watchman,' said the wind. 'I twisted round the weather-cock on the tower and it creaked as if the watchman up there was snoring, only there was no watchman. Rats and mice were the only inhabitants. Poverty laid the table; poverty lurked in wardrobe and larder. The doors fell off their hinges, cracks and crannies appeared everywhere; I went in and out,' said the wind, 'so I know all about it.

'The hair and the beard of Waldemar Daa grew grey, in the sorrow of his sleepless nights, amid smoke and ashes. His skin grew grimy and yellow, and his eyes greedy for gold, the long expected gold.

'I whistled through the broken panes and fissures; I blew into the daughters' chests where their clothes lay faded and threadbare; they had to last for ever. A song like this had never been sung over the cradles of these children. A lordly life became a woeful life! I was the only one to sing in the castle now,' said the wind. 'I snowed them up, for they said it gave warmth. They had no firewood, for the forest was cut down where they should have got it. There was a biting frost. Even I had to keep rushing through the crannies and passages to keep myself lively. They stayed in bed to keep themselves warm, those noble ladies. Their father crept about under a fur rug. Nothing to bite, and nothing to burn! a lordly life indeed! Whew! whew! let it go! But this was what Waldemar Daa could not do.

'"After winter comes the spring," said he; "a good time will come after a time of need; but they make us wait their pleasure, wait! The castle is mortgaged, we are in extremities—and yet the gold will come—at Easter!"

'I heard him murmur to the spider's web.—"You clever little weaver! You teach me to persevere! If your web is broken, you begin at the beginning again and complete it! Broken again—and cheerfully you begin it over again. That is what one must do, and one will be rewarded!"

'It was Easter morning, the bells were ringing, and the sun was at play in the heavens. Waldemar Daa had watched through the night with his blood at fever pitch; boiling and cooling, mixing and distilling. I heard him sigh like a despairing soul; I heard him pray, and I felt that he held his breath. The lamp had gone out, but he never noticed it; I blew up the embers and they shone upon his ashen face, which took a tinge of colour from their light; his eyes started in their sockets, they grew larger and larger, as if they would leap out.

'Look at the alchemist's glass! something twinkles in it; it is glowing, pure and heavy. He lifted it with a trembling hand and shouted with a trembling voice: "Gold! gold!" He reeled, and I could easily have blown him over,' said the wind, 'but I only blew upon the embers, and followed him to the room where his daughters sat shivering. His coat was powdered with ash, as well as his beard and his matted hair. He drew himself up to his full height and held up his precious treasure, in the fragile glass: "Found! won! gold!" he cried, stretching up his hand with the glass which glittered in the sunbeams: his hand shook, and the alchemist's glass fell to the ground shivered into a thousand atoms. The last bubble of his welfare was shattered too. Whew! whew! fare away! and away I rushed from the goldmaker's home.

'Late in the year, when the days were short and dark up here, and the fog envelops the red berries and bare branches with its cold moisture, I came along in a lively mood clearing the sky and snapping off the dead boughs. This is no great labour, it is true, yet it has to be done. Borreby Hall, the home of Waldemar Daa, was having a clean sweep of a different sort. The family enemy, Ové Ramel from Basness, appeared, holding the mortgage of the Hall and all its contents. I drummed upon the cracked window panes, beat against the decaying doors, and whistled through all the cracks and crannies, whew! I did my best to prevent Herr Ové taking a fancy to stay there. Ida and Anna Dorothea faced it bravely, although they shed some tears; Johanna stood pale and erect and bit her finger till it bled! Much that would help her! Ové Ramel offered to let them stay on at the Castle for Waldemar Daa's lifetime, but he got no thanks for his offer; I was listening. I saw the ruined gentleman stiffen his neck and hold his head higher than ever. I beat against the walls and the old linden trees with such force that the thickest branch broke, although it was not a bit rotten. It fell across the gate like a broom, as if some one was about to sweep; and a sweeping there was indeed to be. I quite expected it. It was a grievous day and a hard time for them, but their wills were as stubborn as their necks were stiff. They had not a possession in the world but the clothes on their backs; yes, one thing—an alchemist's glass which had been bought and filled with the fragments scraped up from the floor. The treasure which promised much and fulfilled nothing.

[illegible]

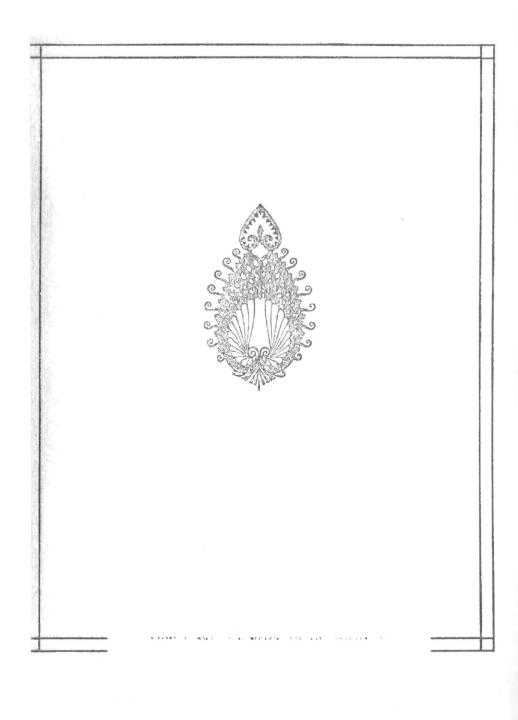

He lifted it with a trembling hand and shouted with a trembling voice: 'Gold! gold!'

2 H

[illegible]

Waldemar Daa hid it in his bosom, took his staff in his hand, and, with his three daughters, the once wealthy gentleman walked out of Borreby Hall for the last time. I blew a cold blast upon his burning cheeks, I fluttered his grey beard and his long white hair; I sang such a tune as only I could sing. Whew! whew! away with them! away with them! This was the end of all their grandeur.

'Ida and Ana Dorothea walked one on each side of him: Johanna turned round in the gateway, but what was the good of that? nothing could make their luck turn. She looked at the red stones of what had once been Marsk Stig's Castle. Was she thinking of his daughters?

'"The elder took the younger by the hand,
And out they roamed to a far-off land."

Was she thinking of that song? Here there were three and their father was with them. They walked along the road where once they used to ride in their chariot. They trod it now as vagrants, on their way to a plastered cottage on Smidstrup Heath, which was rented at ten marks yearly. This was their new country seat with its empty walls and its empty vessels. The crows and the magpies wheeled screaming over their heads with their mocking "Caw, caw! Out of the nest, Caw, caw!" just as they screamed in Borreby Forest when the trees were felled.

'Herr Daa and his daughters must have noticed it. I blew

into their ears to try and deaden the cries, which after all were not worth listening to.

'So they took up their abode in the plastered cottage on Smidstrup Heath, and I tore off over marshes and meadows, through naked hedges and bare woods, to the open seas and other lands. Whew! whew! away, away! and that for many years.'

What happened to Waldemar Daa? What happened to his daughters? This is what the wind relates.

'The last of them I saw, yes, for the last time, was Anna Dorothea, the pale hyacinth. She was old and bent now; it was half a century later. She lived the longest, she had gone through everything.

'Across the heath, near the town of Viborg, stood the Dean's new, handsome mansion, built of red stone with toothed gables. The smoke curled thickly out of the chimneys. The gentle lady and her fair daughters sat in the bay window looking into the garden at the drooping thorns and out to the brown heath beyond. What were they looking at there? They were looking at a stork's nest on a tumble-down cottage; the roof was covered, as far as there was any roof to cover, with moss and house-leek; but the stork's nest made the best covering. It was the only part to which anything was done, for the stork kept it in repair.

'This house was only fit to be looked at, not to be touched. I had to mind what I was about,' said the wind. 'The cottage

Waldemar Daa hid it in his bosom, took his staff in his hand, and, with his three daughters, the once wealthy gentleman walked out of Borreby Hall for the last time.

was allowed to stand for the sake of the stork's nest; in itself it was only a scarecrow on the heath, but the dean did not want to frighten away the stork, so the hovel was allowed to stand. The poor soul inside was allowed to live in it; she had the Egyptian bird to thank for that; or was it payment for once having pleaded for the nest of his wild black brother in the Borreby Forest? Then, poor thing, she was a child, a delicate, pale hyacinth in a noble flower-garden. Poor Anna Dorothea; she remembered it all! Ah, human beings can sigh as well as the wind when it soughs through the rushes and reeds.

'Oh dear! oh dear! No bells rang over the grave of Waldemar Daa. No schoolboys sang when the former lord of Borreby Castle was laid in his grave. Well, everything must have an end, even misery! Sister Ida became the wife of a peasant, and this was her father's sorest trial. His daughter's husband a miserable serf, who might at any moment be ordered the punishment of the wooden horse by his lord. It is well that the sod covers him now, and you too, Ida! Ah yes! ah yes! Poor me! poor me! I still linger on. In Thy mercy release me, O Christ!"

'This was the prayer of Anna Dorothea, as she lay in the miserable hovel which was only left standing for the sake of the stork.

'I took charge of the boldest of the sisters,' said the wind. 'She had clothes made to suit her manly disposition, and took a place as a lad with a skipper. Her words were few and looks stubborn, but she was willing enough at her work. But with all her will she could not climb the rigging; so I blew her overboard before any one discovered that she was a woman, and I fancy that was not a bad deed of mine!' said the wind.

'On such an Easter morning as that on which Waldemar Daa thought he had found the red gold, I heard from beneath the stork's nest a psalm echoing through the miserable walls. It was Anna Dorothea's last song. There was no window; only a hole in the wall. The sun rose in splendour and poured in upon her; her eyes were glazed and her heart broken! This would have been so this morning whether the sun had shone upon her or not. The stork kept a roof over her head till her death! I sang at her grave,' said the wind, 'and I sang at her father's grave. I know where it is, and hers too, which is more than any one else knows.

'The old order changeth, giving place to the new. The old high-road now only leads to cultivated fields, while peaceful graves are covered by busy traffic on the new road. Soon comes Steam with its row of waggons behind it, rushing over the graves, forgotten, like the names upon them. Whew! whew! Let us be gone! This is the story of Waldemar Daa and his daughters. Tell it better yourselves, if you can,' said the wind, as it veered round. Then it was gone.

Text printed by T. and A. Constable, Printers to His Majesty, Edinburgh
Illustrations by Henry Stone and Son, Ltd., Banbury